Scuba
Hand Signals

Pocket Companion for Recreational Scuba Divers

Black & White Edition

LARS BEHNKE

Disclaimer of Liability

Although the author has made every effort to ensure that the information in this book was correct at press time, he does not assume and hereby disclaims any liability to any party for any loss, damage, or injury, including death, caused by errors or omissions, whether such errors or omissions result from negligence, accident, or any other cause.

The information in this book is meant to supplement, not replace, proper scuba diving training. Scuba diving poses some inherent risk. The authors advises readers to take full responsibility for their safety and know their limits.

Never dive without proper training and certification.

© 2015 Lars Behnke
apporiented.com
Version 1.8.4
ISBN-10: 1511614714
ISBN-13: 978-1511614719
Printed by CreateSpace

How to Use QR Codes

Since grayscale photos of colorful reef fish are of limited use, wildlife photos have been replaced by QR codes (Quick Response Codes) in this black & white edition of *Scuba Diving Hand Signals*. Scanning a QR code with your smartphone will open a web browser and a web page that displays a photo of the animal that corresponds to the illustrated hand signal. All you need is a smartphone with camera, an internet connection, and a QR code scanner app. Free QR code scanner apps are available for all common smartphone operating systems.

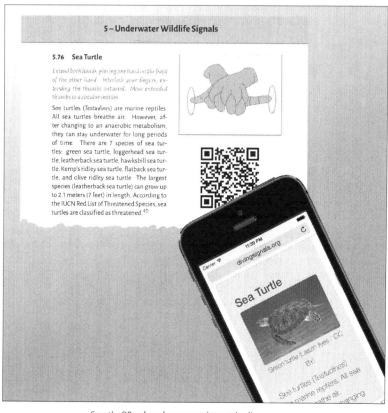

Scan the QR code and access supplemental online resources.

Contents

1	Common Signals	Page 4
2	Problem Signals	Page 17
3	Training Signals	Page 28
4	Air Pressure and Number Signals	Page 32
5	Underwater Wildlife Signals	Page 37
6	Environment Signals	Page 76
7	Emotion Signals	Page 81
8	Miscellaneous Signals	Page 84

1 – Common Signals

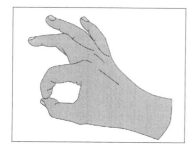

1.1 OK ★

Touch thumb to forefinger in a circle. Extend other fingers.

This is a question–response signal (that is, it is used to both ask a question and give a response). Signaling "Are you OK?" requires a diver's buddy to either reply with the same signal to indicate "yes" or use a different signal to indicate a problem.

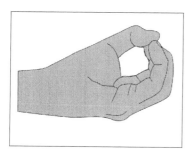

1.2 OK (Gloves) ★

Curl fingers into a loose fist, palm facing up. Touch thumb to forefinger.

Divers wearing thick gloves use this signal as they are generally not able to extend their fingers as required for indicating the standard **OK** signal (section 1.1).

1.3 OK (Surface Signal 1) ★

Shape a large O by reaching both arms overhead with fingertips touching.

Divers use this signal at the surface as it is easier to identify from a distance than is the standard **OK** signal (section 1.1).

1 – Common Signals

1.4 OK (Surface Signal 2) ★

Reach one arm overhead, touching fingertips to the top of head.

Divers use this signal at the surface if a hand is occupied by equipment.

1.5 OK (Light Signal)

Use the light beam of your torch to trace a circle on the ground near your buddy.

This signal is commonly used on night or cave dives, where darkness makes it difficult to identify hand signals. Divers should never direct their light beams directly into their buddies' faces.

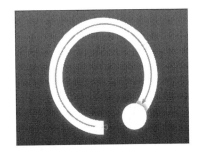

1.6 Stop and Wait ★

Raise hand vertically, keeping fingers together, with your palm facing the diver you are communicating with.

Technical and cave divers typically favor the clenched fist to indicate **Stop**.

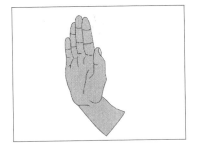

1 – Common Signals

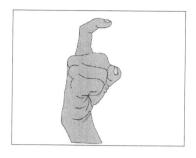

1.7 Question

Clench one hand into a fist, leaving the forefinger extended. Crook the extended forefinger.

Divers use this signal in combination with another signal in order to express a question. For example, a diver can use the **exhausted** signal (section 2.24) followed by the **question** signal in order to ask "Are you tired?"

1.8 Yes

Nod your head.

This signal can be given as an affirmative response to a **question** (section 1.7). Alternatively, signaling **OK** (section 1.1) is also acceptable in many cases.

1.9 No

Shake your head from side to side.

This signal can be given as negative response to a question (section 1.7). Alternatively, some divers use the **don't** signal (section 1.11).

1 – Common Signals

1.10 I Don't Know *

Shrug shoulders and raise palms, bending arms at the elbows.

This signal can be given in response to a question. It can also mean "I don't understand."

1.11 Don't…

Repeatedly shake your raised forefinger from side to side.

The **don't** signal is typically followed by another signal indicating the forbidden action.

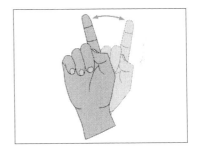

1.12 Descend *

Clench one hand into a fist, leaving the thumb extended and pointing downward.

The **down** signal is a question–response signal. Signaling "Are you ready to descend?" requires a diver's buddy to either reply with the same signal to begin descending or use a different signal to indicate a problem.

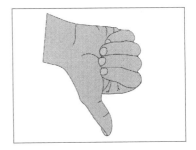

1 – Common Signals

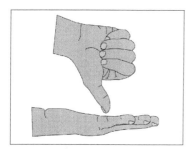

1.13 Descend to Level

Clench one hand into a fist, leaving the thumb extended. Hold the other hand flat, palm facing upward and fingers together. Move the extended thumb of one hand downward against the other hand's flat palm.

This signal is often followed by a signal that indicates a target depth. If no depth is indicated, the signal typically means "Descend to my or the group's level."

1.14 Ascend *

Clench one hand into a fist, leaving the thumb extended and pointing upward.

The **ascend** signal is a question–response signal. Signaling "Are you ready to ascend?" requires a diver's buddy to either reply with the same signal to begin ascending or use a different signal to indicate an alternative suggestion.

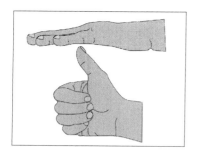

1.15 Ascend to Level

Clench one hand into a fist, leaving the thumb extended. Hold the other hand flat, palm facing downward and fingers together. Move the extended thumb of one hand upward against the other hand's flat palm.

This signal is often followed by a signal that indicates a target depth. If no depth is indicated, the signal typically means "Ascend to my or the group's level."

1 – Common Signals

1.16   Come Here ★

Extend arm away from your body, with palm facing inward. Bending at the elbow, bring arm in toward your body.

Divers use this signal to request a diving buddy to come closer.

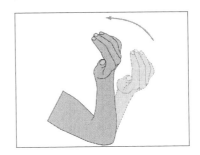

1.17   Look ★

Clench one hand into a fist, leaving the forefinger and middle finger extended and slightly separated. Point with extended forefinger and middle finger to your eyes.

This signal is typically followed by a second signal to express where or at what to look.

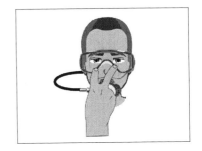

1.18   I (Me) ★

Clench one hand into a fist, leaving the forefinger extended. Point the extended forefinger at your chest.

This signal is accompanied by one or several other signals that express an action.

1 – Common Signals

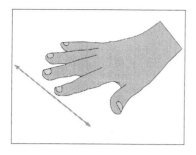

1.19 Level Off (at This Depth) ★

Face palm down and spread fingers. Slowly move your hand back and forth along a horizontal line.

When divers reach their target depth, they use this signal to indicate remaining at the current depth.

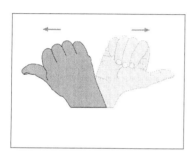

1.20 Which Way? ★

Clench one hand into a fist, leaving the thumb extended. Rotate fist with extended thumb back and forth 180 degrees.

This signal is used to indicate confusion regarding the intended direction in which to swim.

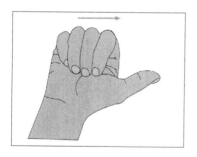

1.21 This Way ★

Clench one hand into a fist, leaving the thumb extended. Point with your extended thumb in the target direction.

Many divers use this signal to alert a diving buddy to the direction in which they intend to swim. Alternatively, some divers use the **this way (CMAS)** signal (section 1.22) to indicate a direction.

1 – Common Signals

1.22 This Way (CMAS)

Hold hand flat and upright, with fingers together, bending arm at the elbow. Lower hand in the target direction.

CMAS divers favor this alternative signal over the standardized **this way** signal (section 1.21).

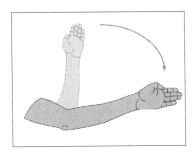

1.23 Dive Over (Above) ★

Face palm down and keep fingers together. Move hand slowly up and forward in a curved motion.

Divers use this signal to indicate the route to go over an underwater obstacle.

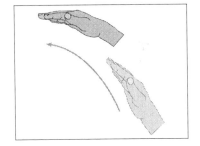

1.24 Dive Under (Below) ★

Face palm down and keep fingers together. Move hand slowly down and forward in a curved motion.

Divers use this signal to indicate the route to go under an underwater obstacle.

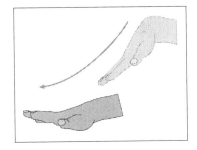

1 – Common Signals

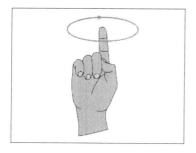

1.25 Turn Around ★

Clench one hand into a fist, leaving the forefinger extended and pointing upward. Trace a circle with the raised forefinger.

Divers use this signal to indicate their intention to turn around and swim back the way they came. Sometimes this signal is accompanied by the signals **home** (section 8.10) or **boat** (section 1.31).

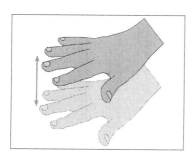

1.26 Relax (Slow Down) ★

Face palm down and spread fingers slightly. Move hand up and down repeatedly.

This signal can be used to tell a nervous or exhausted diver to relax. It is also applicable to request "Please swim slower!"

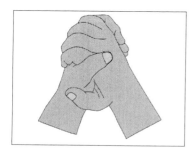

1.27 Hold Hands ★

Clasp your hands together.

Beginning scuba divers sometimes feel uncomfortable or nervous underwater. Holding hands with a dive buddy typically calms a nervous diver down.

1 – Common Signals

1.28 Faster (Hurry Up)

Clasp fingertips together, palm facing upward. Trace a circle with your fingertips repeatedly.

Although recreational scuba diving should be a relaxed activity, there are situations where things have to go fast. Divers use this signal to indicate "Hurry up!"

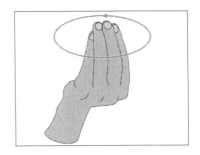

1.29 Lead–Follow ★

Point at the diver who will lead with one hand. Point at the diver who is supposed to follow with the other hand. Move hand indicating the follower behind the hand indicating the leader. Both hands should point in the target direction.

When two or more divers intend to follow an underwater route, one diver should lead the team. This is not necessarily the diver with the most experience in underwater navigation.

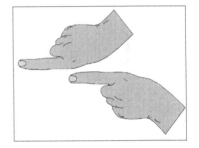

1.30 Remember (Think) ★

Clench one hand into a fist, leaving the forefinger extended. Touch forehead with your extended forefinger. Then move your fingertip up and away from your forehead.

Instructors sometimes use this gesture to ask divers to remember something from class. It is also often used in a more general sense to ask "Remember what we've talked about in our dive briefing."

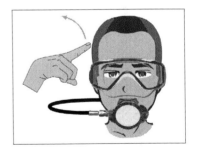

1 – Common Signals

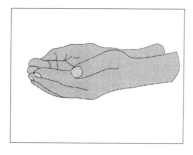

1.31 Boat ★

Cup hands together into a bowl shape, with palms facing upward.

This signal is sometimes used in combination with the **turn around** signal (section 1.25), to express "Let's swim back to the boat." Paired with the **ceiling** signal (section 1.37), divers use it to communicate "Boat above! Watch your head when ascending."

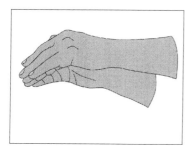

1.32 Wreck

Cup hands together into a bowl shape, with palms facing downward.

This signals is used to indicate a wreck. Recreational open water divers should not dive into wrecks or other overhead environments without specialized training.[7]

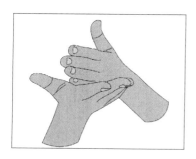

1.33 Navigate

Hold one hand flat and horizontal, palm facing up and fingers together. Place other hand perpendicular to the first, roughly pointing in the target direction.

Divers use this gesture to indicate their intention to follow an underwater route. Although the signal suggests a compass, it does not specify *how* to navigate. Divers commonly use natural navigation or compass navigation.[2]

1 – Common Signals

1.34 This (There)

Clench one hand into a fist, leaving the forefinger extended. Point with the extended forefinger to the object or person of interest.

Divers use this signal to alert a buddy of something. It should not be confused with the **this way** signal (section 1.21).

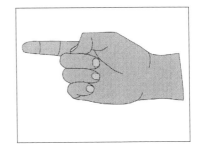

1.35 Ascend, Exit This Way

Clench hand into a fist, leaving the forefinger and thumb extended. Point the extended forefinger toward the exit.

This gesture combines the signals **ascend** (section 1.14) and **there** (section 1.34).

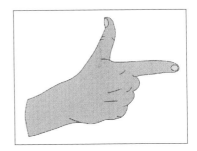

1.36 Safety Stop

Hold one hand flat and horizontal, palm facing down and fingers together. Place other hand underneath and hold up three fingers.

All major dive-training organizations recommend a safety stop. PADI divers make a safety stop for three minutes at five meters before ending a no-decompression dive.

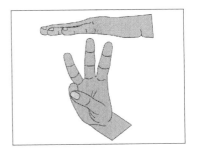

1 – Common Signals

1.37 Ceiling

Hold one hand flat and horizontal, with palm facing down, over the top of your head. Sweep hand back and forth.

Divers use this signal to either indicate that a diver has gone into a decompression obligation or that there is a solid obstruction (for example a boat or cave ceiling) above.

1.38 Pick Me Up

Raise one arm above your head, with fingers clenched into a fist.

Divers use this signal to let the surface team know that they need some support. Typically, it means "Please pick me up!" Since this is not an emergency signal, but rather a request, don't expect the crew to react with urgency.

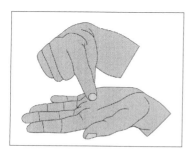

1.39 Write It Down

Hold one hand flat and horizontal, palm facing up and fingers together. Clench the other hand into a fist, leaving the forefinger and thumb extended and touching. Move the extended forefinger and thumb in a randomized pattern across your flat palm.

If all attempts to communicate via hand signals fail, divers use this signal to suggest switching to an underwater writing board.

2 – Problem Signals

2.1 Problem *

Place hand, palm down and fingers spread, against your other arm's forearm. Rock hand back and forth along your palm.

This signal is generally followed by another signal indicating the source of the problem.

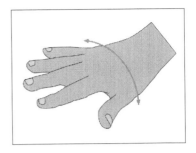

2.2 Problem and Emergency (Light Signal)

Using the light beam of your torch, trace a vertical line several times on the ground next to your buddy.

Most divers use this signal to indicate a problem or emergency.[3] However, some divers prefer tracing horizontal lines for this purpose.[2] Be sure to sort out the meaning of the signal in a dive briefing.

2.3 Help! (Surface Signal) *

Raise one arm straight overhead. Wave extended arm in a 90-degree angle, striking the water surface as arm moves down.

This is an emergency signal. The surface support is directed to start a rescue operation as soon as possible if a diver indicates **help**. Compressed air sirens, whistles, or other noisemakers are also helpful in alerting the surface team.

2 – Problem Signals

2.4 Lost My Buddy

Raise both arms with hands flat and extended upward, palms facing inward, and fingers together.

If divers become separated from their dive buddies, they should search for them for no longer than a minute before surfacing.[1]

2.5 Low on Air ★

Holding one hand several inches in front of your chest, clench hand into a fist. Move fist toward chest.

Although listed here, this signal does not necessarily indicate a problem. When your buddy signals **low on air**, both of you should slowly ascend, make a safety stop, and end the dive.

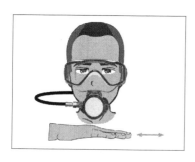

2.6 Out of Air ★

Hand flat, fingers together, and palm down, move your hand in a horizontal line across your throat.

If divers run out of air, they should follow the emergency ascent procedures recommended by their dive organizations.[1,3,4] CMAS divers use a slightly different signal to indicate "out of air". Instead of the cutting motion, they move a horizontally extended hand back and forth in front of their throats.[3,4]

2 – Problem Signals

2.7 Give Me Air *

Remove regulator from mouth. Move fingers of one hand, palm facing your body and fingers together, toward and away from mouth repeatedly.

Divers use this signal to indicate a need for air. A dive buddy should offer his or her octopus regulator immediately. Then, the team should start an alternate air source ascent.[1,4]

2.8 Visible Danger *

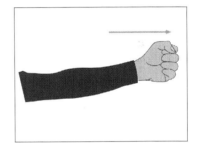

Clench your fingers into a fist. Extend your arm toward the source of danger.

Divers use this signal to alert a dive buddy of a visible danger, for example an aggressive animal. PADI divers use this signal as a general purpose signal for indicating danger.[1]

2.9 Danger *

Clench both hands into fists and cross your forearms in front of your chest.

Divers use this signal to indicate a danger that is not necessarily visible, for example a strong current. It is often followed by another signal indicating the source of danger.

2 – Problem Signals

2.10 Safe

*Signal **danger** (section 2.9). Then bring your forearm in an upright position, leaving your hands clenched into fists.*

This signal is usually used to indicate that a danger is over.

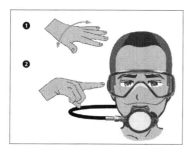

2.11 Ear(s) Not Clearing ★

*Signal **problem** (section 2.1). Then clench one hand into a fist, leaving the forefinger extended. Point forefinger to the ear.*

Divers experiencing problems clearing their ears when descending should ascend a little and try it again. If all attempts to equalize fail, the team should end the dive. If the problem occurs while ascending, it is recommended to descend a few meters and then restart the ascent more slowly.[5]

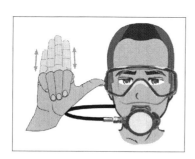

2.12 Ear(s) Not Clearing (CMAS)

With palm facing forward, fingers together, and thumb extended, place your hand next to the problem ear. Open and close your four fingers repeatedly.

CMAS divers use this signal instead of the standard **ears not clearing** signal (section 2.11).[3]

2 – Problem Signals

2.13 Cold ★

Cross arms in front of chest and rub upper arms.

Becoming hypothermic underwater is dangerous for various reasons. It decreases the diver's concentration, attentiveness, and motor skills.[7] Some divers have problems controlling an inflator with numb fingers. Divers who get excessively cold underwater should end the dive.[5]

2.14 Sick

Signal problem (section 2.1). Then place the back of your hand, with fingers spread, on your forehead.

There is a multitude of reasons why divers might feel sick underwater. Most of them should lead the diver to end the dive. Divers who feel nauseated during a dive should know that they can vomit through the regulator if necessary.[7]

2.15 Bitten

Signal problem (section 2.1). Then hold one hand flat, palm facing downward and fingers together. Form a V shape between the thumb and fingers of your other hand and grasp the downward-facing hand in a biting motion.

Injured divers should end the dive and seek medical help. All wounds, no matter what size, should be attended to and monitored for signs of a bacterial infection.[7]

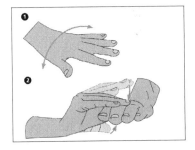

2 – Problem Signals

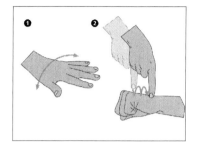

2.16 Stung

*Signal **problem** (section 2.1). Then clench one hand into a fist, holding arm horizontally. Using the extended forefinger of your other hand, tap the back of your horizontal fist in several different places.*

Divers stung by a venomous animal should try to identify the animal that delivered the sting, end the dive, and seek medical consultation. If stung by a jellyfish, applying vinegar[6] or hot water[7] on the affected skin proved to be helpful first aid measures.

2.17 Venomous

Clench both hands into fists, leaving forefingers extended. Cross your extended forefingers under your regulator to suggest skull and crossbones.

Divers use this signal to caution their buddies against a venomous animal. Depending on the potential risk, it is sometimes used in combination with the **danger** signal (section 2.8).

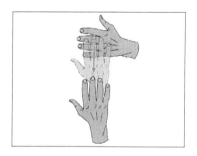

2.18 Bleeding

Hold one hand horizontally in front of your chest, palm facing body, fingers apart. Place your other hand vertically across the first one, palm facing body, fingers apart. Then draw it slowly downward.

This signal is generally followed by another signal indicating the person or body part that is bleeding. Injured divers should end the dive. All wounds should be attended to and monitored for signs of a bacterial infection.[7]

2 – Problem Signals

2.19 Rescue

*Signal **ascend** (section 1.14) with one hand. Then push fist slowly upward with your other horizontally extended hand.*

In rare cases divers may not be able to return to the surface under their own power. Rescue divers use this signal to indicate a rescue operation.

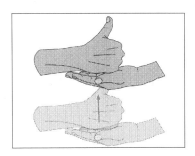

2.20 Decompression Stop

Clench one hand into a fist, leaving the little finger extended.

Recreational scuba divers should not plan a decompression dive.[1] It is important to know this signal, though, in case zero time limits are accidentally exceeded. This signal may be followed by one or more signals indicating the decompression time in minutes.

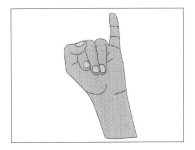

2.21 Fear

Hold hand in front of chest, palm facing body and fingers apart. Shake hand up and down repeatedly.

Divers should know their limits and not hesitate to inform their buddies about concerns or fears they might have during the dive. Don't do anything you are not comfortable with! Alternative signal: Some divers create a claw with a hand and move it in circles close to their hearts.

23

2 – Problem Signals

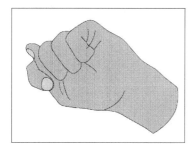

2.22 Stuck

Clench one hand into a fist. Stick your thumb between your forefinger and middle finger.

This signal is generally followed by another signal indicating who or what got stuck.

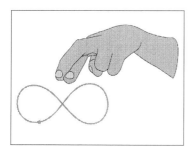

2.23 Entanglement

Clench one hand into a fist, leaving the forefinger and middle finger extended. Cross the extended middle finger over the extended forefinger. Draw a sideways eight repeatedly.

In rare cases divers become entangled in old fishing lines, since they are difficult to see underwater. At some dive sites fishing nets and kelp may impose a danger too. Divers should always carry an appropriate cutting tool when diving at such locations.[7]

2.24 Exhaustion ★

Palms facing your body, place both hands on your chest. Move hands out and in repeatedly.

Since exhaustion can cause cramps or other serious problems, exhausted divers should rest and concentrate on correct scuba breathing until they feel comfortable again.[1,5] It is also recommended to ascend to a shallower depth in order to reduce the regulator's breathing resistance.[3]

2 – Problem Signals

2.25 Dizziness *

Clench one hand into a fist, leaving the forefinger and middle finger extended. Trace circles with the extended fingers.

Divers feeling dizzy underwater should immediately end the dive and seek medical consultation. Alternobaric vertigo can lead to a loss of balance, disorientation, and panic.[7] This signal should not be confused with the **turn around** signal (section 1.25).

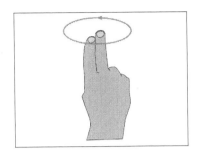

2.26 Nitrogen Narcosis

*Signal **problem** (section 2.1). Clench one hand into a fist, leaving the forefinger extended and pointing at the side of your head. Then trace circles with your forefinger.*

Most divers experience symptoms of nitrogen narcosis on dives greater than 30 meters (100 feet) deep. Nitrogen narcosis often leads to disorientation, poor decision making, and lack of self-control.[7]

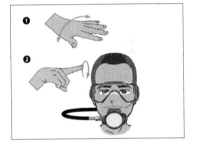

2.27 Big Bubbles

Palm facing upward, open and close fingertips repeatedly.

This signal indicates a leaking piece of equipment. If divers observe a stream of big bubbles coming out of their gear (or their buddies' gear), the buddy team should end the dive and check the leaking piece of equipment.[6]

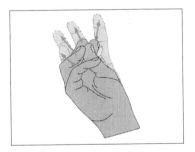

2 – Problem Signals

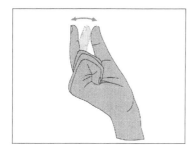

2.28 Tiny Bubbles

Clench hand into a fist, leaving forefinger and thumb extended. Clasp and unclasp extended fingertips repeatedly.

If the stream of bubbles coming out of a piece of gear is very tiny, divers can usually continue their dive but should monitor their air pressure carefully. The gear should be checked after the dive. If the surface of a hose has a leak, no matter how tiny, end the dive, since it may indicate an imminent hose rupture.[6]

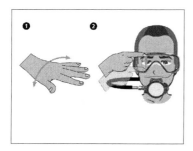

2.29 Mask Flooded

*Signal **problem** (section 2.1). Then clench one hand into a fist, leaving the forefinger extended. Slowly drag the extended forefinger from the bottom to the top of the window glass of your outer mask.*

Water ingress into dive masks is normal to some degree. However, a mask rapidly filling with water can be problematic. If the leak cannot be fixed underwater by adjusting the mask position or by removing hair from under the silicone seal, end the dive.

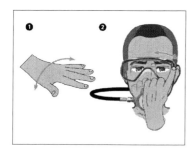

2.30 Mask Foggy

*Signal **problem** (section 2.1). Then clench one hand into a fist, leaving the forefinger extended. Sweep your extended forefinger back and forth across the window glass of your outer mask like a windshield wiper.*

Divers distracted by a foggy mask may put themselves in dangerous situations by losing control of their buoyancy or missing their buddies' signals. Flooding and clearing the mask typically helps for a short period of time.[6]

2 – Problem Signals

2.31 Poor Visibility or Silt Out

Put open palms on your outer mask window as if covering your eyes.

Light failure or stirred up sediment can abruptly reduce underwater visibility or cause a silt out. Unprepared divers run the risk of becoming disoriented or they may loose their buddies.

2.32 Cramp

Open and close the spread-apart fingertips of one hand. Then point to the cramped body part.

A diver suffering from muscle cramps underwater should immediately stretch the affected muscle. If the calf muscle is cramping, grasp the tip of the fin and pull it toward the body while extending the leg.[7]

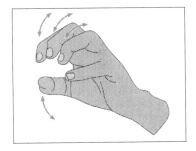

2.33 I Am Lost

Signal I don't know (section 1.10). Then signal navigate (section 1.33).

This signal does not necessarily mean there is a problem as long as at least one member of the buddy team is able to do the navigation.

3 – Training Signals

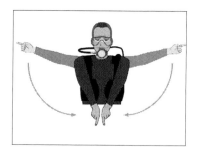

3.1 Gather

Spread arms out to your sides. Clench both hands into fists, leaving the forefingers extended. Move your extended arms down, with forefingers pointing to a spot in front of you.

Before dive instructors start an underwater demonstration or practical exercise, they often use this signal to gather their students.

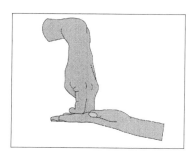

3.2 On Your Knees

Hold one hand out in front of you, palm facing up and fingers together. Push bended forefinger and middle finger of other hand onto the upward-facing hand's palm.

When attending a practical exercise underwater, students should take a stable position on the pool (or sea) bottom that allows them to follow the instructor's demonstration closely.

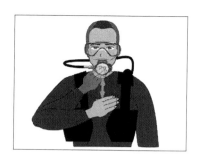

3.3 Breathe

Place one hand on your regulator, palm facing your body and fingers together. Slowly move hand out and in.

Correct scuba breathing is a key skill new divers have to learn. Typically, instructors use this signal to demonstrate deep and slow breathing. In contrast to the gestures in the **give me air** signal (section 2.7), the regulator is not taken out of the mouth and the hand movements are slower.

3 – Training Signals

3.4 Attention!

Clench both hands into fists, leaving the forefingers extended. Point the extended forefingers straight up, palms facing out.

Dive instructors sometimes use this signal to draw the students' attention to a demonstration.

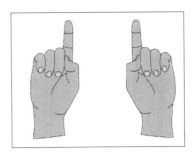

3.5 Exercise Begins

Signal **OK** *(section 1.1) with both hands.*

At times, this signal is used to indicate the start of a demonstration or exercise.

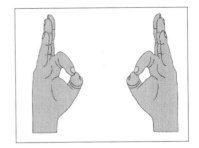

3.6 Exercise Ends or Abort Action

Cross forearms, palms facing down and fingers together. Move hands out to the sides until arms are no longer crossed.

This signal is often used to indicate the end of a demonstration or exercise. It is also applicable more generally to indicate "abort action." See also the **cut** signal (section 8.15).

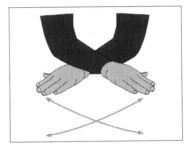

3 – Training Signals

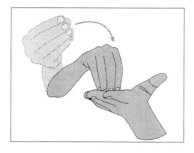

3.7 Again (Repeat)

Hold one hand in front of you, palm facing up and fingers together. Clasp the fingertips of the other hand together. Move the clasped fingertips down to touch the palm of your open hand.

Instructors occasionally use this signal to indicate the repetition of an exercise. It is also applicable more generally to indicate "repeat action."

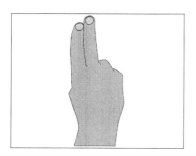

3.8 Buddy

Clench one hand into a fist, leaving the forefinger and middle finger extended. Palm facing your body, point the forefinger and middle finger upward.

This signal is typically used together with other hand signals. For example in combination with the **question** signal (section 1.7), it is used to ask "Where or who is your buddy?"

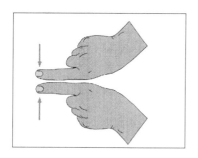

3.9 Get with Your Buddy ★

Clench both hands into fists, leaving the forefingers extended. Hold extended forefingers parallel to each other, slightly apart. Move forefingers slowly together.

The buddy system is a corner stone of dive safety. Yet it only works if dive buddies monitor each other.

3 – Training Signals

3.10 Move Apart

Clench both hands into fists, leaving the forefingers extended. Hold extended forefingers together and parallel to each other. Move forefingers slowly apart.

Dive instructors sometimes use this signal when beginning scuba divers hinder themselves by swimming too close to each other.

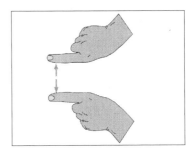

3.11 Ascend a Little

Extend your hand, palm facing up and fingers together. Move hand slowly upward.

Beginners often dive too close to the bottom, stirring up sediments with their fins. Dive guides or instructors typically use this signal to ask students to ascend a little.

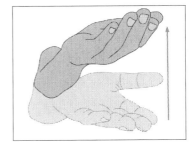

3.12 Lay Down / Hover

Hold forearm horizontally in front of your body, with fingers extended and palm facing down. Place elbow of your other arm upon the extended hand while moving the forearm repeatedly up and down.

Maintaining a neutral buoyancy is an important skill new divers have to learn. If divers have achieved neutral buoyancy they will ascend as they inhale and descend as they exhale.

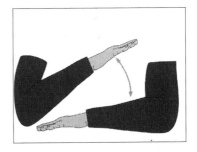

4 – Air Pressure and Number Signals

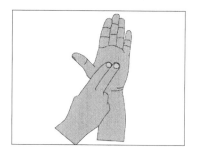

4.1 How much Air?

Hold one hand flat, palm facing outward and fingers together. Place the other hand's extended forefinger and middle finger into the flat hand's palm.

This is a question–response signal. Signaling "How much air?" requires a diver's buddy to reply with his or her current air pressure. Alternative signal: Some divers simply point at their pressure gauge.

4.2 Air Pressure in Bars

While there are several ways to communicate air pressure in bars, this signal is widely used at dive centers around the world.

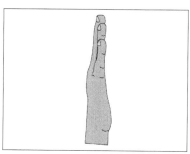

200 bar

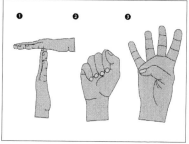

190 bar

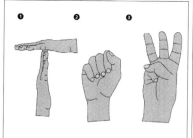

180 bar

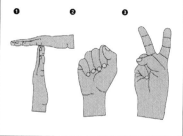

170 bar

4 – Air Pressure and Number Signals

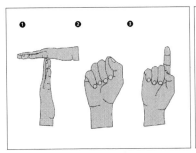

160 bar

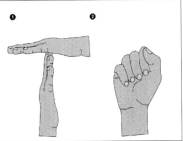

150 bar

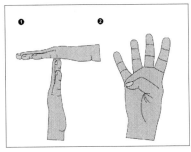

140 bar

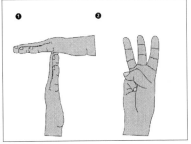

130 bar

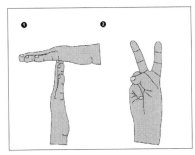

120 bar

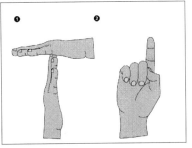

110 bar

4 – Air Pressure and Number Signals

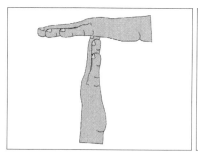
100 bar

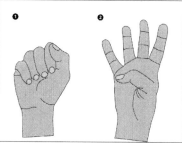
90 bar

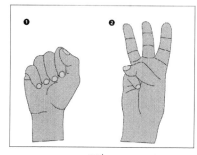
80 bar

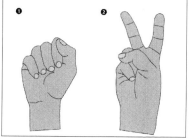
70 bar

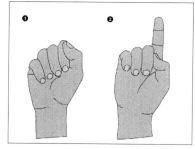
60 bar

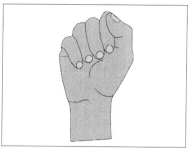
50 bar

4 – Air Pressure and Number Signals

4.3 Air Pressure in PSI

Count off pressure in increments of 100 PSI per finger on one hand. Flash all five fingers for each 500 PSI of remaining air.

While there are various ways to communicate air pressure in PSI, this method is often used by US dive schools.

Examples:

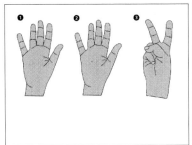
1200 PSI

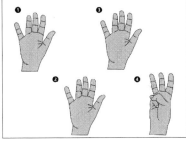
1800 PSI

4.4 Alternative Ways to Indicate Air Pressure

New scuba divers will probably use one of the methods described above. However, some divers, mainly technical and cave divers, prefer to communicate air pressure by indicating the single digits of the pressure value (bar or PSI) one by one from left to right. Sometimes the trailing zero is omitted.

4 – Air Pressure and Number Signals

4.5 Numbers

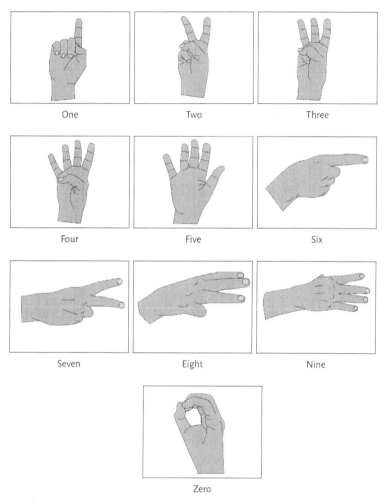

For indicating numbers one through five, raise the corresponding number of fingers with palm facing outward. For indicating numbers six through nine, extend the corresponding number of fingers sideways with palm facing toward your body, where one finger indicates six, two fingers indicate seven, and so forth. For indicating numbers greater than ten, indicate digits one by one from left to right.

5 – Underwater Wildlife Signals

5.1 Kelp (Seaweed)

Hold forearm roughly horizontal, with fingers extended and palm facing down. Hold other forearm upright and place elbow on the back of the extended hand. The move the upright arm slightly back and forth.

Kelp is a marine brown algae of the order *Laminariales*. Growing in coastal waters of colder ocean regions kelp forests form a highly productive ecosystem. The genera *Macrocystis* and *Nereocystis* have a very high growth rate, adding up half a meter per day under optimal conditions. They can reach a total length of 80 meters (260 feet).[19]

5.2 Sponge

Clench both hands into fists. Holding fists together thumb to thumb, rotate one hand clockwise and the other hand counterclockwise.

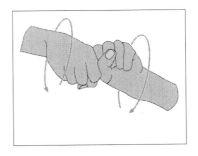

Sponges (*porifera*) are multicellular organisms that consist of cells embedded in a gelatinous matrix and enclosed by two thin layers of epidermal cells. Sponges lack the digestive, nervous, and circulatory systems known from higher organisms. Complex sponges contain a system of channels, pores, and chambers. The shape of the sponge is supported by tiny structural elements (spicules).[14] Upon contact the Caribbean fire sponge (*Tedania ignis*) and some other species can cause a painful rash and a severe itching reaction that lasts for days.[15]

5 – Underwater Wildlife Signals

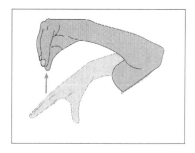

5.3 Jellyfish

Clasping and unclasping your fingertips, move your hand along a vertical line upward.

The jellyfish is the free-swimming life stage of members of the phylum *cnidaria*. Its body consists of a pulsating gelatinous bell and tentacles suspended from its edge. The tentacles are covered with stinging cells (cnidocytes), which are used to capture prey. *Cyanea arctica* can reach 2 meters (6.6 feet) across the body. The sea wasp (*Chironex fleckeri*) and some other species of box jellyfish are infamous for their extremely painful and occasionally fatal stings.[16] The sting of the Portuguese man o' war or bluebottle jellyfish (*Physalia physalis*) can cause pain, fever, vomiting, and unconsciousness in severe cases.[17]

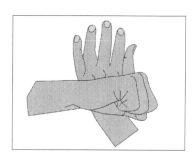

5.4 Coral or Anemone

Hold one hand in front of you, palm facing your body and fingers spread apart. Clench the other hand into a fist. Place your fist against the back of your flat hand.

Sea anemones and corals are cnidarians (*anthozoa*) without free-swimming life stage. While a coral is a colony of myriads of identical polyps, a sea anemone is a single organism. Most corals obtain nutrients from symbiotic photosynthetic algae known as *zooxanthellae*.[14] Skin contact with fire corals (technically no true corals) causes severe pain that can last for several days. Full neoprene or Lycra suits provide adequate protection.[15]

5 – Underwater Wildlife Signals

5.5 Clam

Touch your wrists together, forming small cups with both hands. Bring the fingertips of both hands together, then apart, repeatedly.

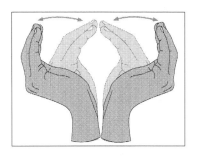

Clams are bivalve mollusks. Two valves connected by a hinge joint form the shell. Like gastropods they have a heart, kidneys, a mouth, a stomach, and a nervous system. However, clams have no heads and are typically blind (except for scallops, which have rudimentary eyes). Most species (oysters and mussels) are attached to substrate and unable to move, while some species (scallops) are able to swim short distances.

5.6 Giant Clam [IP]

With the backs of your hands facing each other, interlock your fingers. Bring your palms together, leaving fingers interlocked.

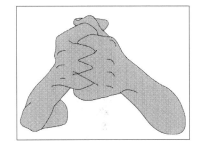

The giant clam is the world's largest extant bivalve mollusk, reaching 120 centimeters (47 inches) across. It has an average lifespan of about one hundred years. Giant clams are filter feeders. Their diet consists of plankton. Symbiotic algae provide them with supplementary nutrients. The giant clam is not considered dangerous to humans.[25]

5 – Underwater Wildlife Signals

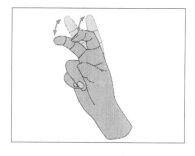

5.7 Sea Slug

Clench one hand into a fist, leaving the forefinger and middle finger extended. Wiggle the extended forefinger and middle finger.

"Sea slug" is the common name for a heterogeneous group of saltwater snails without external shells. The name is applied to members of the clades *Nudibranchia* (a prominent group of colorful gastropods), *Sacoglossa* (sap-sucking sea slugs), and *Aplysiomorpha* (large animals with small, proteinaceous internal shells).

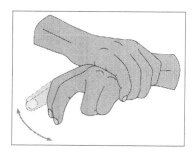

5.8 Sea Snail

Use one hand to clasp the back of your other hand. Clench the covered hand into a fist, leaving the forefinger and middle finger extended. Wiggle the extended forefinger and middle finger together.

Sea snails are marine gastropods. In contrast to sea slugs, they typically have coiled shells. *Syrinx aruanus*, the largest living sea snail, reaches 91 centimeters (36 inches) in length. Most sea snails do not pose a threat to divers. However, the venomous tooth of some cone snail species can be dangerous and even fatal. In severe cases victims have suffered muscle paralysis, changes in vision, and respiratory failure. The tooth can penetrate neoprene.[6]

5 – Underwater Wildlife Signals

5.9 Cowry

Clench both hands into fists. Bring fists together, with the backs of the hands facing outward.

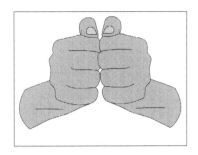

Egg-like shells are characteristic for this group of sea snails. The smooth and shiny shells have been used as currency by African indigenous people for centuries. The Atlantic deer cowry (*Macrocypraea cervus*) reaches 19 centimeters (7.5 inches) in length. However, most species are much smaller.

5.10 Octopus

Place the wrist of one hand under your chin, fingers pointing down. Wiggle your fingers.

The octopus has eight arms (four pairs). Its body is bilaterally symmetrical and lacks an internal or external skeleton. A chitin beak (similar to a parrot's beak) is the only hard part of the body. Octopuses have highly developed nervous systems that make them the most intelligent of all invertebrates. Potentially dangerous to divers are blue-ringed octopuses. Their venom is potent enough to kill a human.

5 – Underwater Wildlife Signals

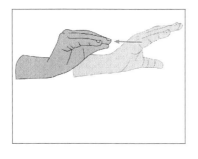

5.11 Squid ()

Clasping and unclasping your fingertips, move your hand along a horizontal line.

Squids are soft-bodied and generally have eight powerful arms and two long tentacles for catching prey. Like octopuses they have a highly developed nervous system. In contrast to octopuses, their mantle has two swimming fins along each side. Furthermore, the sucker rings of squids are armed with extra hooks that provide additional gripping power. Squids range from 2.5 centimeters (1 inch, *Idiosepius sp.*) to 20 meters (7.9 feet, giant squid) in length.

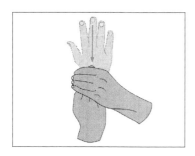

5.12 Christmas Tree Worm

Hold one hand upright, palm facing your body and fingers spread apart. Lightly grab wrist with your other hand. Retract your upright hand downward through the grasp of your other hand.

The sedentary Christmas tree worm has a segmented body that is typically anchored in a tubular burrow. Only two modified prostomial palps are visible from the outside. These small spiral structures (3.8 centimeters or 1.5 inches in span) are brightly colored and resemble Christmas trees. The worm uses the spirals for feeding and respiration. When disturbed, they are rapidly retracted into the burrow.

5 – Underwater Wildlife Signals

5.13 Shrimp or (Spiny) Lobster

Clench both hands into fists, leaving the forefingers extended. Place hands on both sides of your head and wiggle the extended forefingers.

Shrimps (or prawns) are slender crustaceans that are well adapted for swimming. The ventral part of their long muscular abdomen supports pleopods (swimming legs). With their robust legs, lobsters and spiny lobsters are well adapted for walking on the ocean floor. In contrast to crabs, they do not walk sideways. Spiny lobsters lack the large claws. In general, lobsters are 25–50 centimeters (10–20 inches) long.

5.14 Cleaner Shrimp

*Signal **shrimp** (section 5.13). Put open palm on your cheek. Move your hand in circles as if cleaning your face.*

Cleaner shrimps are a heterogenous group of crustaceans that live in cleaning symbiosis with larger fish. Fish benefit from this relationship by getting rid of ectoparasites and debris, while cleaner shrimps obtain nutrients. Cleaner shrimps are commonly reef associated and establish cleaning stations, that are visited by client fish on a regular basis.

5 – Underwater Wildlife Signals

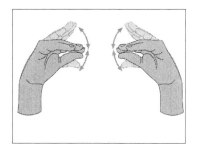

5.15 Crab

Clasp and unclasp the fingertips on both hands simultaneously.

Crabs are characterized by a pair of claws, a thick external skeleton, and a reduced abdomen, usually hidden under the thorax. They have eight robust legs, which are well adapted for walking on the seafloor. Unlike lobsters, crabs typically walk sideways. Their sizes range from a few millimeters in width (pea crab) to 4 meters (13 feet, Japanese spider crab).

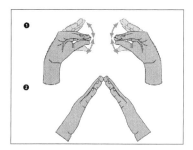

5.16 Hermit Crab

*Signal **crab** (section 5.15). Then hold hands at an angle, with palms flat, fingers together, and fingertips touching.*

Hermit crabs carry around empty seashells, which give them shelter. Growing crabs must change their shells on a regular basis. The size of hermit crabs ranges from a few millimeters to 10–20 centimeters (3.9–7.8 inches, *Coenobita brevimanus*).

5 – Underwater Wildlife Signals

5.17 Stingray (♛)

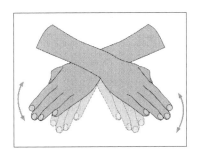

Cross forearms, with palms flat and fingers together. Move both hands together slowly up and down.

Stingrays (*Dasyatidae*) are a group of rays characterized by barbed and venomous stingers near their tails. A stinger can reach 35 centimeters (14 inches) in length and is used exclusively in self-defense. A stingray's sting usually causes inflammation, pain, and muscle cramps and tends to get infected from bacteria. Typically, injuries are not life threatening if no vital organ is affected. Most species of stingrays are found on the seafloor of coastal waters. They prefer sandy surfaces, which they can hide in. Coral reefs are popular feeding grounds. Some stingrays, such as eagle rays, live in open water.

5.18 Bluespotted Ribbontail Ray or Bluespotted Stingray ♛ IP

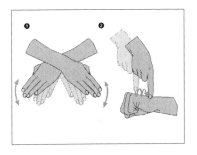

Signal stingray (section 5.17). Then dapple with the extended forefinger of one hand some spots on the back of the other hand.

Although similar in appearance and name, the bluespotted stingray and the bluespotted ribbontail ray are two distinct species. The bluespotted stingray is olive green and covered with blue spots. Its angular body reaches a width of 50 centimeters (20 inches). A bluespotted stingray's tail has white markings at its tip.[11] Its sting can be deadly to humans.[26] The bluespotted ribbontail ray has a yellowish back with blue spots and a tail with blue stripes. Its body is round and reaches 90 centimeters (3 feet) in length.[11] The bluespotted ribbontail ray delivers a sting that is painful but usually not fatal.

5 – Underwater Wildlife Signals

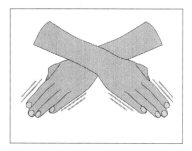

5.19 Electric Ray

Cross forearms, with palms flat and fingers together. Shake your hands as if suffering from an electric shock.

Electric rays are a group of rays capable of producing an electric discharge of anywhere from 8 to 220 volts. The electricity is used to stun prey, but it is also used for self-defense. An electric ray's body typically consists of a broad and nearly circular disc, a short snout, and a short, thick tail. The shock delivered by the marbled electric ray is seldom deadly to humans but can be very painful.

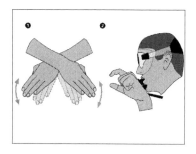

5.20 Eagle Ray

Signal stingray (section 5.17). Then clench one hand into a fist, leaving the forefinger crooked. Place your hand in front of your nose.

Eagle rays (*Myliobatidae*) have rhomboidal bodies and long tails. Some species, such as manta rays, can occasionally be observed leaping out of the water into the air.[8] Eagle rays live in open water.

5 – Underwater Wildlife Signals

5.21 Manta Ray

Extend both arms fully to the sides. Move arms up and down repeatedly.

Manta rays (*Manta sp.*) are large eagle rays with triangular pectoral fins and long head fins. *Manta birostris* reaches a width of 7 meters (23 feet). Mantas have the largest brain–to–body mass ratio of all sharks and rays. They do not carry a sting and are not dangerous to divers.

5.22 Shark

Place an upright hand, palm flat and fingers together, against your forehead.

Sharks are cartilaginous fish related to rays. They are characterized by 5 to 7 gill openings on the sides of their heads and by pectoral fins that are not connected to their heads. The dwarf lantern shark (*Etmopterus perryi*) is the smallest species, reaching only 17 centimeters (7 inches) in length. The largest shark is the whale shark (*Rhincodon typus*), which reaches about 12 meters (39 feet) in length. The majority of sharks feed on other fish. Large sharks prey on marine mammals as well. Most species do not impose a threat to divers. Shark attacks are typically motivated out of curiosity or mistaken identity. In most cases, after a single sample bite, the shark retreats.[9] Like most wild animals, sharks will usually defend themselves if provoked.

5 – Underwater Wildlife Signals

5.23 Reef Shark [IP]

Signal shark (section 5.22). Then signal coral (section 5.4).

Several species of reef-associated sharks are known as reef sharks: the blacktip reef shark, the Caribbean reef shark, the grey reef shark, and the whitetip reef shark.[9] Typically, reef sharks are easily frightened away by swimmers and scuba divers, but some unprovoked attacks on humans have been reported. In particular, grey reef sharks (8 unprovoked attacks) and blacktip reef sharks (11 unprovoked attacks) should be regarded as potentially dangerous.[10]

5.24 Hammerhead Shark

Clench both hands into fists. Place hands on both sides of your forehead.

The hammerhead shark (*Sphyrnidae*) is characterized by a flattened and laterally extended cephalofoil that makes its head look like a hammer. The function of this shape is not fully understood, but sensory reception and maneuvering seem likely. Hammerhead sharks range from 0.9 meters (3 feet) to 6 meters (19.7 feet) in length. The scalloped, great, and smooth hammerheads have been reported to attack humans. As of 2013, 17 unprovoked incidents (all nonfatal) have been reported.[10]

5 – Underwater Wildlife Signals

5.25 Leopard Shark [EP]

Place an upright hand, palm flat and fingers together, against your forehead. Then dapple some spots with your other hand's forefinger on the side of your upright hand.

Leopard sharks (*Triakis semifasciata*) are easily identified by their prominent pattern of black markings and large spots on their grayish backs. Adult females can reach 1.8 meters (5.9 feet) in length. Males are usually smaller.[9] Leopard sharks are considered harmless to humans, if not provoked.[10]

5.26 Bull Shark

*Signal **shark** (section 5.22). Then place hands, fingers together and at a 90-degree angle to the palms, on both sides of your head.*

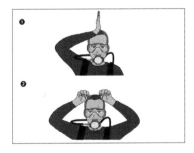

Bull sharks (*Carcharhinus leucas*) have stout bodies and long caudal fins. They reach about 3.4 meters (11 feet) in length and 315 kilograms (694 pounds) in weight. Bull sharks have the highest bite force of all sharks. They are considered dangerous to humans (93 unprovoked attacks, 26 fatal).[10] Bull sharks are probably responsible for the majority of fatal shark attacks on humans (mainly swimmers) in tropical coastal waters.[9]

5 – Underwater Wildlife Signals

5.27 White Shark

*Signal **shark** (section 5.22). Then add to this signal by creating the same signal with your other hand and placing it on top of the first.*

Great white sharks (*Carcharodon carcharias*) are the largest living predatory fish on the planet, reaching 6.4 meters (21 feet) in length. Their upper bodies are grayish, and their underbellies are white. Their streamlined, torpedo-shaped bodies make them fast swimmers, reaching a top speed of 56 kilometers (35 miles) per hour.[27] White sharks are dangerous to humans and should be considered such by divers. As of 2013, 279 unprovoked attacks (78 fatal) on humans have been reported.[10] On the IUCN Red List, the white shark is classified as vulnerable.[9]

5.28 Oceanic Whitetip Shark

*Signal **shark** (section 5.22). Then extend both arms fully to the sides.*

The oceanic whitetip shark (*Carcharhinus longimanus*) has a stocky body and long rounded fins with white tips. Adult sharks can reach a length of more than 3 meters (9.8 feet). They live in the open sea far from the coasts and prefer tropical and warm-temperate waters.[9] Oceanic whitetip sharks are considered aggressive and are suspected to be responsible for many fatal attacks on survivors of downed aircrafts and sunken ships.[28] Since these attacks are unconfirmed, they are not included in the International Shark Attack File.[10]

5 – Underwater Wildlife Signals

5.29 Nurse Shark [EP A]

*Signal **shark** (section 5.22). Then clench one hand into a fist, leaving the forefinger and middle finger extended. Place the extended forefinger and middle finger against the side of your neck.*

Nurse sharks (*Ginglymostoma cirratum*) have a yellow- to gray-brown body, strong jaws, and distinctive tail fins that can be up to one-fourth their total length. In contrast to most other sharks, nurse sharks have smooth skin. They reach about 3 meters in length.[9] Some divers have been attacked after approaching a sleeping animal. In total, 10 unprovoked attacks on humans (all non-fatal) have been reported.[10]

5.30 Thresher Shark

*Signal **shark** (section 5.22). Then clasp together the fingertips on both hands. Touch the fingertips together, holding one hand on top of the other. Move your top hand upward in a large arc.*

The thresher shark (*Alopias sp.*) is easily identified by its large eyes and its whiplike caudal fin that can be as long as its entire body. Thresher sharks range from 3 meters (9.8 inches) to 6.1 meters (20 feet, common thresher, *Alopias vulpinus*) in length and feed on schooling pelagic fish, squid, and cuttlefish. Thresher sharks use their tails as weapons to stun or kill prey.[9] They are considered harmless to divers.[10]

5 – Underwater Wildlife Signals

5.31 Tiger Shark

Signal shark (section 5.22). Then clench one hand into a fist, leaving three fingers extended. Place your fist, palm facing inward, against your opposite shoulder.

A juvenile tiger shark (*Galeocerdo cuvier*) is easily identified by the dark stripes on its body. This pattern fades as the shark matures. Tiger sharks can reach 5.5 meters (18 feet) in length. Underwater they are usually not aggressive toward scuba divers.[9] Yet, 101 unprovoked attacks (28 fatal) on humans have been reported as of 2013.[10]

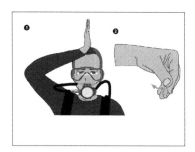

5.32 Sandtiger Shark [IP A]

Signal shark (section 5.22). Then signal sand (section 6.8).

Sandtiger sharks (*Carcharias taurus*) are also known as raggedtooth sharks or grey nurse sharks. They have light brown bodies with dark spots. The two dorsal fins are similar in size. The tail fin is extremely asymmetrical. Sandtiger sharks inhabit coastal waters of warm temperate to tropical regions. They can reach 4.3 meters (14 feet) in length.[9] Although their ragged, needle—like teeth give sandtigers a fearsome appearance, no fatal attacks on humans have been reported as of 2013.[10]

5 – Underwater Wildlife Signals

5.33 Whale Shark

*Signal **shark** (section 5.22). Then move one hand, with palm facing down and fingers together, along a horizontal wavy line.*

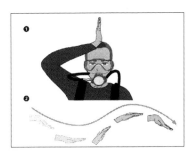

Whale sharks (*Rhincodon typus*) are the largest living fish. They reach a length of 12 meters (39 feet). However, according to unconfirmed reports, much larger animals have been observed.[8] The whale shark has a flattened head and a very large mouth with small, scalelike teeth. Its back and sides are gray to brown with white spots among pale vertical and horizontal stripes, and its belly is white. As a filter feeder, the shark eats plankton and small fish. Whale sharks are harmless to humans.[10] On the IUCN Red List, they are classified as vulnerable.[9]

5.34 Barracuda

Extend one arm, palm facing down and fingers together. Suggest chopping your extended arm into three or four pieces.

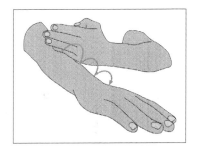

The barracuda (*Sphyraena sp.*) has a slender, streamlined body and a large mouth with a jutting lower jaw and large teeth. Its small scales are smooth to the touch. Their coloration is typically brownish or bluish gray. Their backs may have several dark bars. Barracudas can reach up to 1.8 meters (5.9 feet) in length. At times they attack humans.[8] Divers should remove shiny items like rings or jewelry before entering water inhabited by barracudas, because these items are sometimes mistaken for prey.[17]

5 – Underwater Wildlife Signals

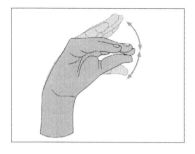

5.35 Moray Eel

Hold hand upright, bending arm at the elbow. Bend your wrist. Clasp and unclasp your fingertips repeatedly.

Moray eels (*Muraenidae*) have slender, prolonged, scaleless bodies and large mouths with numerous fang-like teeth. They range from 11.5 centimeters (4.5 inches, *Anarchias leucurus*)[29] to 4 meters (13 feet, slender giant moray)[30] in length. Moray eels are not aggressive to divers. However, some species will bite if provoked.[17]

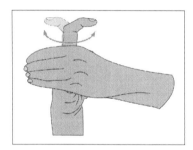

5.36 Garden Eel

Hold one hand upright and clench it into a fist, leaving the forefinger crooked. Lightly grab the fist with your other hand. Then rotate the fist back and forth repeatedly.

Garden eels (*Heterocongrinae*) have slender bodies and small mouths with jutting lower jaws. Pectoral fins are either absent or reduced. Garden eels typically form colonies on sandy bottoms. Their front bodies can often be observed hovering above the bottom, whereas their tails are anchored in the sand. When an animal is disturbed, it retracts its body rapidly into the burrow.[8] Garden eel species usually range from 40 centimeters (16 inches) to 70 centimeters (27.5 inches) in length. They feed on plankton.[11]

5 – Underwater Wildlife Signals

5.37 Angelfish [IP]

Clench one hand into a fist, leaving the forefinger extended. Using the extended forefinger, trace a halo over your head.

Angelfish (*Pomacanthidae*) have colorful, laterally compressed bodies. In contrast to butterflyfish, they are armed with strong spines on their gill covers.[8] Size varies greatly among the different species, ranging from 6 centimeters (2.4 inches, *Centropyge multicolor*) to 50 centimeters (19.7 inches, yellowbar angelfish or *Pomacanthus maculosos*) in length.[12] Note that the name "angelfish" is ambiguous, since other unrelated groups are sometimes named angelfish too, such as the freshwater angelfish, tropical cichlids, Atlantic pomfret, angel shark, ringstraked guitarfish, and Atlantic spadefish.[32]

5.38 Grouper

With both arms, one over the other, grab opposite shoulders. Raise and lower your top elbow repeatedly.

Groupers (*Epinephelinae*) have stout bodies, large heads, and mouths with jutting lower jaws. They have strong tooth plates that are well adapted for crushing prey. Most grouper species carry spines along the front part of their dorsal fins. Some species (giant grouper, potato grouper) reach 2 meters (6.5 feet) in length.[12] Groupers are usually not aggressive. However, at places where divers regularly feed fish, larger grouper species have been reported to bite.[31]

5 – Underwater Wildlife Signals

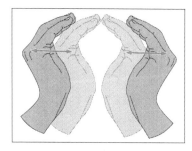

5.39 Pufferfish

Create a C shape with each hand. Bring hands together, with fingertips touching. Move hands apart and together repeatedly.

Pufferfish (*Tetraodontidae*) have the remarkable ability to inflate themselves with water to an enormous size when threatened. This behavior is supposed to discourage potential predators. Their skin is scaleless and elastic. Some species produce the poison tetrodotoxin which can be fatal to humans when taken up with food. Puffers range between 11 centimeters (4.3 inches, sharpnose puffer) and 120 centimeters (47 inches, star puffer) in length.[12]

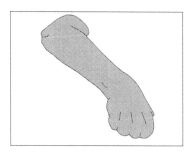

5.40 Boxfish (Cofferfish) (☣)

Clench one hand into a fist. Hold fist at your side, arm slightly away from your body and elbow slightly bent, as if carrying a suitcase.

Boxfish (*Ostraciidae*) are characterized by bony polygonal plates that give them the appearance of a box or suitcase. They have small mouths with conical, stout teeth. Boxfish are poor swimmers. *Acanthostracion quadricornis* can reach a length of 60 centimeters (24 inches). Most species are smaller, though. *Ostracion lentiginosus* and some other boxfish species secrete a highly toxic substance (ostracitoxin) when disturbed,[8] so divers should avoid touching them.

5.41 Longhorn Cowfish [IP]

Clench one hand into a fist, leaving the forefinger and little finger extended.

The longhorn cowfish (*Lactoria cornuta*) is a boxfish (section 5.40) that is easily identified by two horns protruding from its head. It can reach 46 centimeters (18 inches) in length. The longhorn cowfish blows away bottom sand and feeds on exposed benthic invertebrates. It inhabits shallow coastal waters and prefers muddy or sandy sea bottoms.[12]

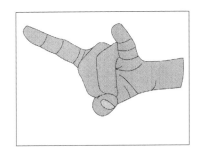

5.42 Butterfish

Hold one hand extended, palm facing upward. Clench the other hand into a fist. Move your fist back and forth across your flat palm as if spreading butter on a slice of bread.

The butterfish (*Stromateidae*) is characterized by a very deep, compressed body and a short snout that is about equal to the eye diameter. Adults do not have pelvic fins.[8] The name "butterfish" is ambiguous, as some unrelated species carry the name too, such as *Odax pullus* (a weed whiting species) and *Psenopsis anomala* (Japanese butterfish).[34]

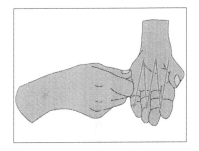

5 – Underwater Wildlife Signals

5.43 Cardinalfish

Hold hands at an angle, with palms flat, fingers together, and fingertips touching, over your head.

Cardinalfish (*Apogonidae*) are relatively small fish with brightly colored bodies and two separated dorsal fins. Most cardinalfish species are less than 15 centimeters (5.9 inches) in length. Many species are mouth breeders, with males carrying eggs and hatchlings in their mouth cavities. Cardinalfish are typically nocturnal, feeding on zooplankton and small benthic invertebrates. Most species are reef associated.[11]

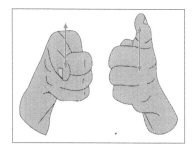

5.44 Drumfish

Clench both hands into fists, leaving forefingers extended and pointing forward. Then move forefingers repeatedly up and down as if playing a drum.

The drumfish (*Scianidae*), also called drum or croaker, has a long dorsal fin with a deep notch between the spinous and soft portion. Drumfish use their swim bladder as resonance chamber for producing drumming sounds. The largest species (*Totoaba macdonaldi*) can grow up to 2 meters (6.6 feet) in length and 100 kilograms (220 pounds) in weight. However, most species are much smaller.[33]

5 – Underwater Wildlife Signals

5.45 Goatfish

Clench one hand into a fist, leaving the forefinger and middle finger extended and slightly apart. Place wrist of fist under your chin, extended fingers pointing down.

The goatfish (*Mullidae*) has an elongated body, a deeply forked caudal fin, and two widely separated dorsal fins. Goatfish are typically brightly colored. Two independently movable barbels are used to detect food buried in sandy substrate.[8] The largest species (dash-dot goatfish, *Parupeneus barberinus*) reaches 50 centimeters (19.7 inches) in length.[11]

5.46 Clownfish (Anemonefish) [IP]

Make an O shape with the fingers of one hand. Place it in front of your nose to suggest a clown nose.

Anemonefish or clownfish (*Amphiprioninae*) are relatively small, ranging between 6 centimeters (2.3 inches, tomato anemonefish) and 17 centimeters (6.7 inches, orange-finned anemonefish) in length. They are commonly colored yellow, orange, or red with white patches or bars. Clownfish live in small hierarchical groups of one large dominant female and several smaller males. If the female dies, the largest male will change its gender and become the group's reproductive female. Clownfish live in symbiosis with certain species of sea anemones.[11]

5 – Underwater Wildlife Signals

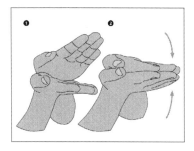

5.47 Flathead [IP]

Hold palms together horizontally. Maintaining contact at the bases of your palms, open and close hands repeatedly.

The flathead (*Platycephalidae*) has an elongated body and a long flattened head with bony ridges, spines, and a large mouth. Its body is covered with a pattern of green, brown, or gray blotches. Flatheads range from 13 centimeters (5.1 inches, spiny flathead) to 47 centimeters (18.5 inches, crocodile flathead) in length. They are a bottom-dwelling species that prefer the sand or rubble substrates of shallow reefs.[11] Flatheads are harmless to humans.

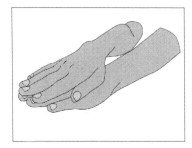

5.48 Flatfish

Extend both hands, placing one hand on the back of the other hand.

Flatfish (*Pleuronectiformes*) are a group of demersal fish with asymmetric bodies. In the course of their development, one eye migrates to the other side of the head. Flatfish lie on their eyeless side buried in sandy substrate, waiting for potential prey. The order of flatfish includes flounders, soles, halibut, turbot, and other popular food fish.[8] The Atlantic halibut (*Hippglossus hippoglossus*) is the largest known species. It can reach a total body length of up to 4.7 meters (15.4 feet).[35]

5 – Underwater Wildlife Signals

5.49 Cornetfish (Flutemouths)

Hold hands out in front of mouth, one in front of the other. Move fingers as if playing a flute.

Cornetfish (*Fistulariidae*) are a family of fish with silver-colored and extremely elongated bodies, long tubular snouts, and tail filaments. They grow to a length of 1.8 meters (5.9 feet). Cornetfish can be found in open water or near coral reefs.[8] They feed on small fish, crustaceans, and other invertebrates.[12]

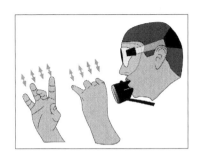

5.50 Hawkfish

Clench one hand into a fist, leaving the forefinger crooked. Place your hand in front of your nose.

Hawkfish have stout to moderately elongated, often colorful bodies, and large heads. The scientific name, *Cirrhitidae*, derives from a set of cirri that are attached near the tips of ten dorsal fin spines. Hawkfish species normally range from 7 centimeters (2.8 inches, dwarf hawkfish) to 28 centimeters (11 inches, halfspotted hawkfish) in length. They can be found on the branches of soft and hard corals or sponges.[11]

5 – Underwater Wildlife Signals

5.51 Jawfish

Clench your hands into fists, leaving the forefingers extended. Place your extended forefingers on your jaw.

Jawfish (*Opistognathidae*) have elongated bodies and relatively large heads and mouths. Most species range from 9 centimeters (3.5 inches, solor jawfish) to 45 centimeters (17.7 inches, Darwin jawfish) in length.[11] Jawfish inhabit sandy bottoms near reefs where they excavate burrows, which give them protection from predators. Jawfish are mouth breeders.[12]

5.52 Rabbitfish IP

Clench one hand into a fist, leaving the forefinger and middle finger extended and slightly apart. With palm facing your head, place fist against the back top part of your head to suggest bunny ears.

Rabbitfish (*Siganus sp.*) have colorful oval bodies with small terminal mouths. They are equipped with venomous dorsal, ventral, and anal spines. Rabbitfish range from 16 centimeters (6.3 inches, masked rabbitfish) to 53 centimeters (20.9 inches, Java rabbitfish) in length. Their diet consists of algae and sea grasses. Some species feed on sponges. Their venom causes severe pain, but it is not fatal to adult humans.[11]

5 – Underwater Wildlife Signals

5.53 Spadefish (Batfish)

Hold both hands flat and fingers together with thumbs overlapping. Move both hands together up and down.

Spadefish (*Ephippidae*, also known as batfish) are characterized by disk-shaped, compressed bodies and typically one or two dark, vertical bars running across the front part of their flanks. The dorsal, anal, and ventral fins of juvenile fish are greatly elongated. The longfin spadefish (*Platax teira*) can reach 41 centimeters (16.1 inches) in length.[11]

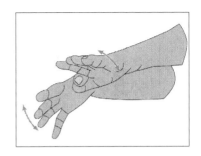

5.54 Butterflyfish

Align extended hands parallel to each other with fingers together and palms facing down. Then move the hand's outer edges up and down repeatedly.

Butterflyfish (*Chaetodontidae*) typically have colorful, highly compressed bodies with dark bands running across their eyes. Many species have eyespots on the rearmost part of their flanks. Their tail fins are never forked. In contrast to angelfish, butterflyfish do not have spines on their gill covers. Butterflyfish can reach 24 centimeters (9.4 inches, dotted butterflyfish) in length.[11]

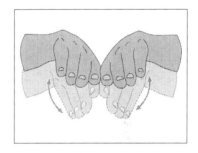

5 – Underwater Wildlife Signals

5.55 Bannerfish IP

Clench both hands into fists, leaving the forefingers and thumbs extended. Form a rectangle at chest level by bringing together the extended fingertips. Draw both hands outward to the edges of your chest.

Bannerfish (*Heniochus sp.*) are a subgroup of the butterflyfish family. They typically have black-and-white banded bodies and yellow caudal and dorsal fins. The longfin bannerfish can reach a maximum length of about 25 centimeters (10 inches). Bannerfish feed on zooplankton, coral polyps, or bottom-dwelling invertebrates.[12]

5.56 Masked Bannerfish IP

Clench both hands into fists, leaving the forefingers and thumbs extended. Form a rectangle at mask level by bringing together the extended fingertips. Draw both hands outward to the edges of your mask.

The masked bannerfish (*Heniochus monoceros*) has a flattened, black-and-white banded body. Its caudal, dorsal, and anal fins are yellow, and its head is marked by a black bar with white blotches or lines.[11] The masked bannerfish reaches a maximum length of about 23 centimeters (9.1 inches) and feeds on bottom-dwelling invertebrates, preferably annelid worms.[12]

5 – Underwater Wildlife Signals

5.57 Moorish Idol [IP]

Holding one hand flat and fingers together, touch the top of your head with your fingertips. Draw a large arc up and away from your head.

The Moorish idol (*Zanclus comutus*) is a common reef fish with a disk-shaped, compressed body. The flanks are banded black and white or yellow. The dorsal fin is prolonged into a trailing filament. The Moorish idol can reach a maximum length of about 16 centimeters (6.3 inches).[11]

5.58 Parrotfish

Place the back of your hand in front of your mouth. Bring the fingers and thumb together and apart repeatedly to suggest a mouth talking.

Parrotfish (*Scaridae*) are named for their parrotlike beaks, which are used for rasping algae from the skeletons of dead coral. Parrotfish species range from 19 centimeters (7.5 inches, raggedtooth parrotfish) to 80 centimeters (32 inches, spotted parrotfish) in length.[11] After nightfall some species, including the queen parrotfish (*Scarus vetula*), form a cocoon by secreting mucus from their mouths. This "sleeping bag" most likely hides their scent from potential predators.[36]

5 – Underwater Wildlife Signals

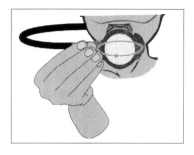

5.59 Sweetlip (Grunt)

Clasp fingertips and thumb together. Trace an outline of your lips.

Sweetlips (*Haemulidae*) are characterized by their thick fleshy lips. They resemble snappers, but are generally smaller and have no fang–like teeth. Sweetlips are also called "grunts" in many regions because they make noises by grinding their teeth plates.[11] Note that the common sweetlip emperor (*Lethrinus miniatus*) is not a member of the sweetlip family, but of the emperors (*Lethrinidae*).

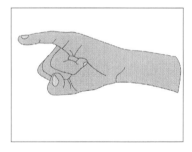

5.60 Pipefish

Hold arm horizontally. Clench one hand into a fist, leaving the little finger extended.

The pipefish has an elongated, slender body encircled by bony rings. It is named for its pipe–like snout. Like seahorses, most pipefish species are poor swimmers. Pipefish typically range from 5 centimeters (2 inches, velvet ghost pipefish) to 40 centimeters (15.7 inches, slender pipefish) in length. They are commonly found in sheltered areas of coral reefs or sea grass areas. Pipefish males incubate the eggs, which are attached to an external brood pouch.[11]

5 – Underwater Wildlife Signals

5.61 Seahorse

Clench both hands into fists, leaving forefingers extended. Use one extended forefinger to hook the other.

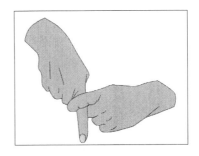

Seahorses (*Hippocampus sp.*) share many features with the closely related group of pipefish. They have slender to stout bodies, flexible necks, and elongated snouts. Their skin is stretched over bony rings. Seahorses do not have scales. They range from 0.5 centimeters (0.2 inches, Severns' pygmy seahorse) to 30 centimeters (11.8 inches, spotted seahorse) in length.[11,12] Like pipefish they are poor swimmers. The dwarf seahorse (*Hippocampus zosterae*) is the slowest-swimming fish in the world, reaching a top speed of about 1.5 meters (5 feet) per hour.[37]

5.62 Lionfish

Interlock fingers, leaving arms angled and fingers extended.

Lionfish (*Pterois sp.*) are members of the scorpionfish family. They are characterized by elongated, feather-like fin rays. Their coloring of red, white, or black bands warns potential predators against their venomous spines. Most species range from 12 centimeters (5 inches, pygmy lionfish) to 45 centimeters (18 inches, longspine lionfish) in length.[11] Lionfish are infamous for their venomousness. A sting causes extreme pain and is sometimes fatal to humans. If provoked, the lionfish swims with erected dorsal spines toward its enemy.[15]

5 – Underwater Wildlife Signals

5.63 Scorpionfish

Interlock fingers, leaving arms angled and fingers extended. Put your hands over your head.

Scorpionfish (*Scorpaenidae*) commonly have stout bodies with large heads adorned with ridges and spines. Their dorsal fin rays are coated with venomous mucus. Typically scorpionfish lie motionless and well camouflaged on the sea bottom, waiting for potential prey. They range from 5 centimeters (2 inches, minor scorpionfish) to 36 centimeters (14.2 inches, tassled scorpionfish) in length.[12] Scorpionfish are considered dangerous to humans. The symptoms of a sting vary from an uncomfortable prickle to intense pain, swelling, diarrhea, nausea, and headaches.[17]

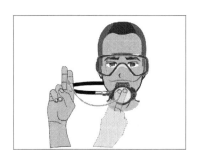

5.64 Stonefish IP

Clench one hand into a fist, leaving forefinger and middle finger extended. Place the extended fingers in front of your mouth. Rotate hand outward and sideways as if smoking a cigarette.

The stonefish, a member of the scorpionfish family, is characterized by its stout body, widely separated bulging eyes, and an upturned mouth. It typically lies motionless and half-buried in the sediment of coastal waters and is easily mistaken for a stone covered with algae. It can reach 35 centimeters (13.8 inches) in length. The stonefish is the world's most venomous fish and is responsible for many human fatalities. The venomous dorsal fin spines are able to penetrate the sole of a tennis shoe.[12]

5 – Underwater Wildlife Signals

5.65 Triggerfish

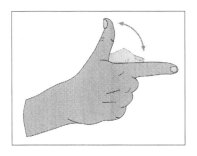

Clench one hand into a fist, leaving forefinger and thumb extended. Lower and raise the thumb repeatedly as if firing a gun.

Triggerfish (*Balistidae*) have compressed bodies and small eyes that are set far back from the terminal mouth. A unique feature of this family are their two-part dorsal fin spines. The first spine is stout and erectable. The second spine locks the erected first spine and allows the fish to wedge itself inside a crevice if threatened by a predator.[38] Triggerfish can reach 75 centimeters (29.5 inches, titan triggerfish) in length. Triggerfish will attack divers who approach their nesting areas.[12] The strong teeth of larger triggerfish species can inflict serious wounds.

5.66 Surgeonfish

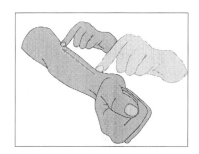

Clench one hand into a fist, leaving the forefinger extended. Use the extended forefinger to draw a line up your other arm's forearm.

The surgeonfish (*Acanthuridae*) has an oval, brightly colored body and characteristic scalpel-like caudal spines. Its continuous dorsal and anal fins are relatively long. Its mouth is small and has a single row of teeth. Surgeonfish species range from 13 centimeters (5 inches, pale-tailed bristletooth) to 1 meter (39 inches, whitemargin unicornfish) in length. If provoked, surgeonfish may use their razor-sharp caudal spines, which can inflict nasty cuts, in self-defense.[11,12]

5 – Underwater Wildlife Signals

5.67 Unicornfish

Clench one hand into a fist, leaving the forefinger extended. Place your fist on your forehead, palm facing outward and extend forefinger upward.

Unicornfish (*Naso sp.*) are relatively large members of the surgeonfish family. The unicornfish is named for a protruding spike or bulbous on its forehead that develops with age.[8] Like other surgeonfish, unicornfish usually have razor-sharp spines near their tail fins, which they also use in self-defense. The whitemargin unicornfish can grow up to 1 meter (39 inches) in length.[11]

5.68 Frogfish (Anglerfish)

Clench one hand into a fist, leaving the forefinger extended. Place fist to the side of your forehead. Wiggle the extended forefinger.

Frogfish (*Antennariidae*) have globular bodies and large upturned mouths. Most species are extremely well camouflaged, and some can change colors. A frogfish attracts potential prey by wiggling its first dorsal spine, which has evolved into a thin antenna tipped with a lure. Their ventral and pectoral fins have evolved into hand–like extremities. Frogfish range from 4.5 centimeters (1.8 inches, Randall's frogfish) to 30 centimeters (11.8 inches, giant frogfish) in length.[11]

5 – Underwater Wildlife Signals

5.69 Monkfish (Goosefish)

Hold both hands flat with fingers together. Touch fingertips and thumbs of one hand to the other hand's. Bring all fingers together and apart repeatedly to suggest the animal's large mouth.

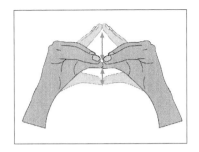

Monkfish (*Lophiidae*) have flattened bodies and very large upturned mouths. Like frogfish (their smaller relatives), the monkfish attracts potential prey by wiggling its first dorsal spine, which has evolved into a thin antenna tipped with a lure. Monkfish can grow up to 1.2 meters (47 inches) in length. However, most species are smaller.[8]

5.70 Trumpetfish [A]

Simulate playing the trumpet.

The trumpetfish (*Aulostomidae*) has an elongated body, a long tubular snout, and a small upturned mouth. Trumpetfish can grow up to 1 meter (40 inches, *Aulostomus maculatus*) in length[12] and they inhabit shallow coastal waters up to a depth of about 120 meters (393 feet). Typically found near reefs and in weedy areas, trumpetfish sometimes swim vertically (snout-down) among branching gorgonians or corals.[11]

5 – Underwater Wildlife Signals

5.71 Sergeant Major [A] or Soldierfish

With hand flat, palm facing downward, and fingers together, hold one hand to the side of your forehead as if saluting.

This signal is ambiguous in tropical regions of the Atlantic Ocean, where many divers use it to indicate the sergeant major. In other regions of the world, divers use this signal to indicate the soldierfish, which belongs to a different family.

The sergeant major (píntano, *Abudefduf saxatilis*) is characterized by its brightly banded sides. It reaches 15 centimeters (6 inches) in length and tends to be found in tropical regions of the Atlantic Ocean.[12] Sergeant majors are highly territorial. Despite their small size, they sometimes attack and chase divers who approach their nesting areas.[17]

Soldierfish and the closely related squirrelfish constitute the family *Holocentridae*. They are reddish in color and have large eyes. Soldierfish are distinguished by their blunt snouts and the missing preopercular spines.[12] They typically range from 15 centimeters (6 inches, East Indian soldierfish) to 32 centimeters (12.6 inches, brick soldierfish) in length.[11] Soldierfish inhabit the coastal waters of the tropical Atlantic, Indian, and Pacific oceans.[8]

5 – Underwater Wildlife Signals

5.72 Humphead Wrasse (Napoleonfish) [IP]

Clench one hand into a fist. Place your fist on your forehead.

The humphead wrasse (*Cheilinus undulatus*) is characterized by distinct thick lips and a bulbous hump on its forehead. Its body is blue or greenish. Males reach 229 centimeters (90 inches) in length, while females are generally smaller. The humphead wrasse plays an important role in the coral reef ecosystem, since it is one of the few species that preys on crown-of-thorn starfish and other toxic animals.[12] Despite their large size, humphead wrasses are typically friendly toward divers. The species is classified as endangered on the IUCN Red List.[20]

5.73 Tuna or Mackerel

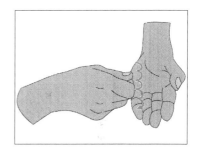

Hold one hand flat, palm facing upward and fingers together. Rotate your fist repeatedly, moving left to right along the side of your open hand as if opening a tuna can.

Tunas and mackerels constitute the family *Scombridae*. Members of this family have streamlined bodies, 2 dorsal fins, 5 to 12 finlets, and deeply forked caudal fins with at least two keels. The pelvic fins are located below the pectoral fins. Tunas are excellent swimmers, reaching a top speed of about 75 kilometers (47 miles) per hour.[39] Size varies greatly among the different species, ranging from 35 centimeters (14 inches, long-jawed mackerel)[11] to 4.2 meters (13.8 feet, bluefin tuna)[8] in length. Due to commercial fishing pressure, the bluefin tuna is classified as endangered on the IUCN Red List.[21]

5 – Underwater Wildlife Signals

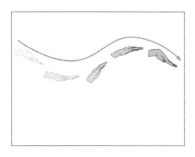

5.74 Whale

Hold hand flat, palm facing downward and fingers together. Move hand along a horizontal wavy line.

Whales are marine mammals. Instead of vertical caudal fins, they have horizontal flukes. Whales must surface periodically to breathe through their nasal openings (blowholes) located on the tops of their heads. The blue whale is the largest living animal on Earth, reaching 33 meters (110 feet) in length. Baleen whales (*Mysticeti*) are filter feeders. Their diet is comprised of small organisms, mainly krill. Baleen whales have two blowholes. In contrast, toothed whales (*Odontoceti*) have only a single blowhole. Larger fish and squid, which are located via echolocation, comprise their main food source.[13]

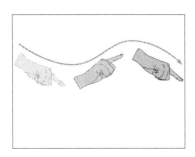

5.75 Dolphin

Clench hand into a fist, palm facing downward, leaving the forefinger extended. Move hand along a horizontal wavy line.

Dolphins (*Delphinidae*) are toothed whales with torpedo-shaped bodies and cleaved flukes. Their forelimbs have evolved into flippers. Dolphins range from 1.4 meters (4.6 feet, Hector's dolphin) to 9 meters (30 feet, orca) in length. Dolphins generally interact well with humans, and their behavior is sometimes even playful.[13]

5 – Underwater Wildlife Signals

5.76 Sea Turtle

Extend both hands, placing one hand on the back of the other hand. Interlock your fingers, extending the thumbs outward. Move extended thumbs in a circular motion.

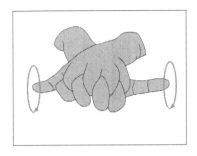

See turtles (*Testudines*) are marine reptiles. All sea turtles breathe air. However, after changing to an anaerobic metabolism, they can stay underwater for long periods of time. There are 7 species of sea turtles: green sea turtle, loggerhead sea turtle, leatherback sea turtle, hawksbill sea turtle, Kemp's ridley sea turtle, flatback sea turtle, and olive ridley sea turtle. The largest species (leatherback sea turtle) can grow up to 2.1 meters (7 feet) in length. According to the IUCN Red List of Threatened Species, sea turtles are classified as threatened.[40]

5.77 Sea Snake 🕱 IP

Clasp together the fingertips of one hand, with palm facing downward. Move hand forward along a wavy line.

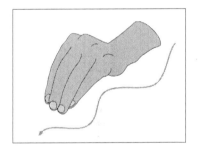

Sea snakes (*Hydrophiinae*) are characterized by laterally flattened bodies and oar-like tails. They are typically black with alternating gray, blue, or white bands. Sea snakes belong to the elapid family (*Elapidae*). As compared to their terrestrial relatives, they have relatively small fangs. Sea snakes must surface regularly to breathe air but can stay submerged for several hours. The largest sea snake species (*Hydrophis spiralis*) grows up to 3 meters (9.8 feet) in length.[41] Snakes provoked by humans will bite in self-defense. The venom of some species can be lethal. Divers can protect themselves by wearing a full neoprene wet suit (6 millimeters).[15]

6 – Environment Signals

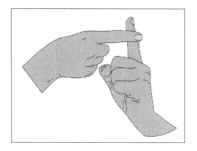

6.1 Temperature

Clench both hands into fists, leaving forefingers extended. Create a T shape with the extended forefingers.

This signal is followed by number signals indicating the temperature in Celsius or Fahrenheit.

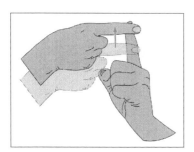

6.2 Temperature Rising

*Signal **temperature** (section 6.1). Then move your horizontal forefinger slowly upward.*

Sometimes this signal is followed by number signals indicating the temperature in Celsius or Fahrenheit.

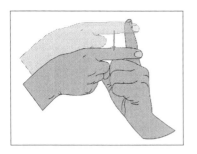

6.3 Temperature Falling

*Signal **temperature** (section 6.1). Then move your horizontal forefinger slowly downward.*

Sometimes this signal is followed by number signals indicating the temperature in Celsius or Fahrenheit.

6 – Environment Signals

6.4 Thermocline

*Signal **temperature** (section 6.1). Then move your horizontally extended forefinger outward in an arc.*

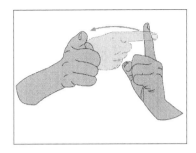

The thermocline is a thin layer in the ocean (or any other large body of fluid) in which water temperature changes rapidly. Sometimes scuba divers can not only feel, but also see this layer which has the appearance of winkled glass.

6.5 Current

Hold one hand flat and vertical, palm facing sideways and fingers together. Form a 90-degree angle with the other hand. Move the horizontally extended fingers of your one hand toward the palm of your vertically extended hand.

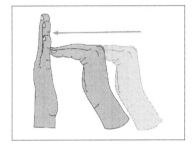

The speed of the movement indicates the strength of the current—the faster you perform the movement, the stronger the indicated current.

6.6 Shallow

Hold forearm at a 45 degree angle in front of your body, with fingers extended and palm facing down. Clench other hand into a fist, leaving forefinger extended. Point with forefinger at the fingertips of your extended hand.

6 – Environment Signals

6.7 Deep

Hold forearm roughly at a 45 degree angle in front of your body, with fingers extended and palm facing down. Clench other hand into a fist, leaving forefinger extended. Point with forefinger at the elbow of your diagonal forearm.

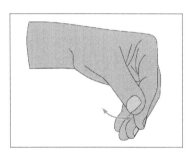

6.8 Sand or Sediment

Rub your thumb against the tips of forefinger and middle finger.

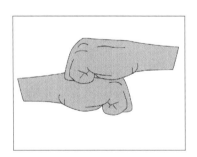

6.9 Stone or Rock

Clench both hands into fists, with back of hands facing upward. Place one fist on top of the other.

Some divers use this signal also to indicate a **stonefish** (section 5.64).

6 – Environment Signals

6.10 Cave or Arc

Create a C shape with one hand. Clench the other hand into a fist, leaving forefinger extended and pointing to opening of the C shape. Move forefinger in circles.

Recreational open water divers should not dive into caves or other overhead environments without specialized training.[7]

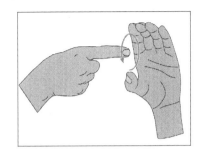

6.11 Drop-Off

Hold one hand horizontally and the other hand vertically, fingertips touching.

Divers use this signal to caution their buddies against a steep downward slope.

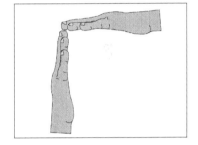

6.12 Bridge or Jetty

Hold one forearm roughly horizontal. Clench other arm's hand into a fist, leaving forefinger and middle finger extended and slightly separated. Using an arc motion, move this hand along the horizontal forearm.

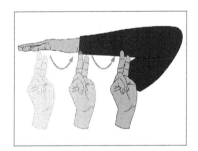

6 – Environment Signals

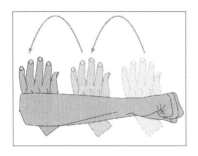

6.13 Coral Reef

Hold one forearm horizontally in front of you. Using an arc motion, move your other hand, palm facing toward your body and fingers spread apart, along your forearm.

Coral reefs are typically created from calcium carbonate secreted by stony corals. They form highly diverse ecosystems. Coral reefs cover less than 0.1 percent of the world's ocean floor. However, they provide a habitat for 25 percent of all marine species.[23] Typically, a water temperature of 26–27 degrees Celsius (79–81 degrees Fahrenheit) is required for stony corals to grow (and reefs to build up).[24]

6.14 Cleaning Station

Put open palm on your cheek. Move hand in circles as if cleaning your face.

A cleaning station is a site where cleaner shrimps or cleaner fish regularly meet larger client fish to rid them of parasites in exchange for nutrients. This kind of relationship is called a cleaning symbiosis.

7 – Emotion Signals

7.1 Love

Holding hands in front of you, touch palms together and crook all four fingers while extending your thumbs downward. Bring fingertips of both hands together to suggest a heart.

This signal is sometimes used to express affection toward something divers are seeing or experiencing.

7.2 Aggressive

Clench both hands into fists. Punch them against each other at shoulder level.

Divers use this signal to caution their buddies against an aggressive animal. Depending on the potential risk, it is sometimes used in combination with the **danger** signal (section 2.8).

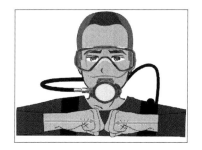

7.3 LOL (Laugh Out Loud)

Make an L shape with each hand (one hand will have the palm facing outward; the other hand will have the palm facing toward you). Hold your hands to the left and right of your regulator.

Since it is hard to laugh underwater without spitting out the regulator, divers typically prefer using this signal if they feel the need to laugh.

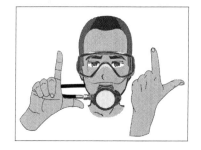

7 – Emotion Signals

7.4 Happy

Clasp together the fingertips of both hands. Touch the fingertips of one hand to those of the other hand in front of your regulator. Draw hands outward and upward, stopping at cheekbone level to suggest a broad smile.

7.5 Sad

Clasp together the fingertips of both hands. Touch the fingertips of one hand to those of the other hand in front of your regulator. Draw hands outward and downward to suggest a sad face.

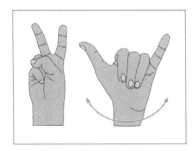

7.6 Too Cool

*Indicate the number **two** (section 4.5). Then clench your hand into a fist, leaving thumb and little finger extended. Rotate your hand back and forth.*

The shaka sign ("hang loose" gesture) was originally adopted by surfers from the Hawaiian culture. However, it is also popular among scuba divers. Usually it is used to express "That's cool!" or "I'am having a good time!"

7 – Emotion Signals

7.7 Boring

Clench one hand into a fist, leaving the forefinger extended. Then suggest picking your nose.

7.8 Whatever (I Don't Care)

Clench both hands into fists, leaving the forefingers and thumbs extended. Touch the tips of the thumbs together, creating a W shape.

Some divers use this signal to indicate that something is not worth the time and energy.

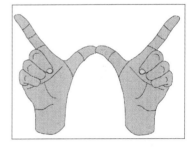

8 – Miscellaneous Signals

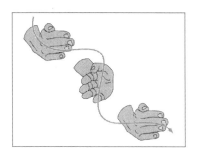

8.1 Fish

Hold one hand flat and roughly horizontal, with fingers together and palm facing sideways. Then move hand along a horizontal wavy line.

8.2 Big

Extend both arms fully to the sides to suggest something big.

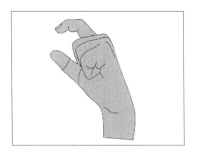

8.3 Small

Clench one hand into a fist, keeping forefinger and thumb extended and slightly apart, to suggest that something is tiny.

8 – Miscellaneous Signals

8.4 Male

Hold hands flat and at a downward angle, palms facing each other and fingers together. Trace a large V shape.

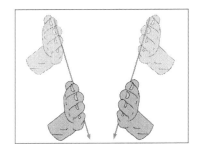

8.5 Female

Hold hands flat and perpendicular to the ground, palms facing each other and fingers together. Move hands along a vertical wavy line.

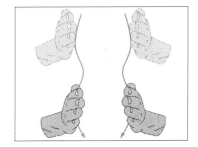

8.6 Mating

Signal **love** (section 7.1). Then turn both hands so your arms are horizontal, and clasp your fingers.

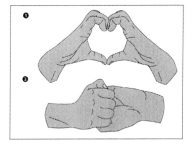

8 – Miscellaneous Signals

8.7 Sleeping

Put palms together. Place your hands next to your ear and slightly bend your head sideways.

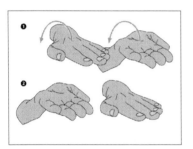

8.8 Dead

Hold hands flat in front of your body, with one palm facing up and one palm facing down. Then turn both hands to opposite positions.

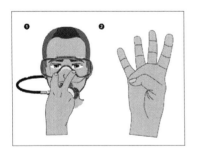

8.9 Search for...

*Signal **look** (section 1.17). Then signal **four** (section 4.5).*

This signal should be followed by additional signals to express what to search for.

8 – Miscellaneous Signals

8.10 Turn Around and Swim Back

*Signal **back** (section 1.25). Then hold hands at an angle, with palms flat, fingers together, and fingertips touching, to suggest a roof.*

This signal is used to communicate swimming back to the entry location. When diving from a boat, the **home** signal is often replaced by the **boat** signal (section 1.31).

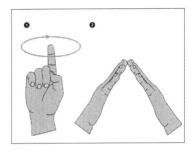

8.11 In Charge

Clench one hand into a fist, leaving three fingers extended. Place your fist, palm facing inward, against your opposite shoulder.

8.12 Swim

Clench one hand into a fist, leaving the forefinger and middle finger extended. Wiggle the extended fingers up and down independently while moving your hand along a horizontal line.

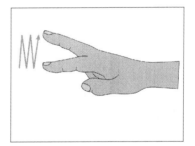

8 – Miscellaneous Signals

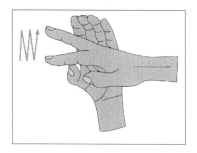

8.13　Swim Through

*Create a C shape with one hand. Signal **swim** (section 8.12) with the other hand, moving through the C-shaped hand.*

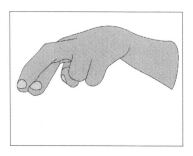

8.14　Line

Clench one hand into a fist, leaving the forefinger and middle finger extended. Cross the middle finger over the forefinger.

Divers use this signal to indicate a rope or (anchor) line. It is used typically in combination with other signals, such as **entanglement** (section 2.23), **cut** (section 8.15), **hold** (section 8.16), or **bind** (section 8.17).

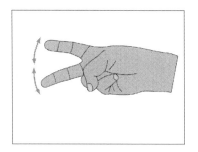

8.15　Cut

Clench one hand into a fist, leaving the forefinger and middle finger extended and spread apart. Move forefinger and middle finger together and apart repeatedly to suggest scissors.

Although this gesture typically means **cut**, some divers use it to indicate their intention to abort an action. See also the **abort** signal (section 3.6).

8 – Miscellaneous Signals

8.16 Hold (Hang On)

Clench both hands into fists. Hold one on top of the other in front of your chest to suggest clutching a vertical line.

If diving in a current, dive guides often use this signal to ask their groups to hang on anchor (or decent) lines during safety (or decompression) stops.

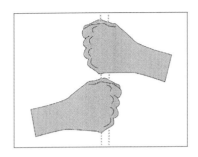

8.17 Bind (Fix)

Clasp both hands into fists. Rotate forearms around each other on a horizontal axis to suggest winding a line.

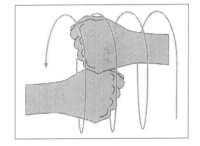

8.18 Knife

Clench one hand into a fist, leaving the forefinger and middle finger extended.

This signal is typically used in combination with other signals, for example **cut** (section 8.15). Note that the knife signal is similar to the **buddy** (section 3.8) and **seven** (section 4.5) signals. However, in most cases it won't be a problem guessing the meaning from context.

8 – Miscellaneous Signals

8.19 Touch

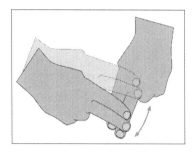

Clench both hands into fists, leaving forefingers and middle fingers extended. Then stroke one hand's extended fingers with the other hand's extended fingers.

8.20 Don't Touch

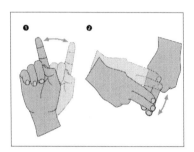

*Signal **don't** (section 1.11). Then signal **touch** (section 8.19).*

Responsible divers should avoid contact with marine creatures and stick to the rule of "look, don't touch."[1, 4]

8.21 Take Photo

Clench both hands into fists, leaving the forefingers and thumbs extended. Form a rectangle at mask level, positioning hands on either side of your mask to suggest a camera. Move extended forefinger down as if pressing the release button.

8 – Miscellaneous Signals

8.22 Battery Full?

Clench one hand into a fist, leaving the forefinger and thumb extended and slightly apart. Clench the other hand into a fist, leaving the forefinger extended. Move the extended forefinger up and down between the extended forefinger and middle finger of your other hand.

This signal is generally followed by an indication of which device is being referred to.

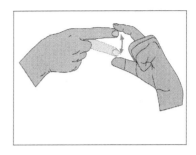

8.23 Battery Full

Clench one hand into a fist, leaving the forefinger and thumb extended and slightly apart. Clench the other hand into a fist, leaving the forefinger extended. Touch the extended forefinger to the other hand's forefinger.

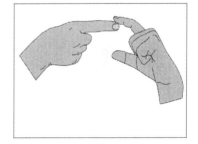

8.24 Battery Half-Full

Clench one hand into a fist, leaving the forefinger and thumb extended and slightly apart. Clench the other hand into a fist, leaving the forefinger extended. Place the extended forefinger halfway between the other hand's forefinger and thumb.

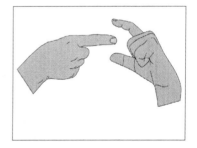

8 – Miscellaneous Signals

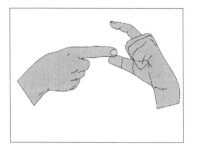

8.25 Battery Low

Clench one hand into a fist, leaving the forefinger and thumb extended and slightly apart. Clench the other hand into a fist, leaving the forefinger extended. Touch the extended forefinger to the other hand's thumb.

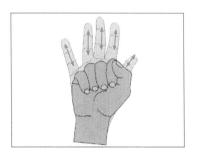

8.26 Light (Lamp)

Raise hand, palm facing outward and fingers slightly apart. Open and close hand repeatedly.

This signal often simply means "light." Cave divers use it to draw their buddies' attention to their reserve lights.

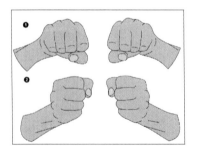

8.27 Broken

Clench both hands into fists, holding hands horizontally and slightly apart. Turn fists vertically to suggest breaking a stick.

Notes

- ★ Formally standardized by the Recreational Scuba Training Council[18]
- IP Inhabits the Indo-Pacific Ocean
- EP Inhabits the East Pacific Ocean
- A Inhabits the Atlantic Ocean
- 🕱 Venomous
- (🕱) Some species venomous

References

[1] *Open Water Diver Manual*. Rancho Santa Margarita: PADI, 2010. Print.

[2] *Adventures in Diving: Manual*. Rancho Santa Margarita: PADI, 2006. Print.

[3] Kromp, T.; Roggenbach, H.; Bredebusch, P. *Praxis des Tauchens*. Delius Klasing, 2014. Print.

[4] Ellerby, D. (BSAC). *The Diving Manual: An Introduction to Scuba Diving*. London: Compass Press Limited, 2004. Print.

[5] Brylske, A. *The Complete Diver: The History, Science and Practice of Scuba Diving*. Parkville: Dive Training Magazine, 2012. Print.

[6] Agnew, J. *Scuba Diver's Travel Companion*. Guilford: The Globe Pequot Press, 2003. Print.

[7] Orr, D.; Douglas, E. *Scuba Diving Safety*. Champaign: Human Kinetics, 2007. Print.

[8] Nelson, J. *Fishes of the World (4th edition)*. Hoboken, New Jersey: John Wiley & Sons, 2006. Print.

[9] Compagno, L.; Dando, M.; Fowler, S. *Sharks of the World*. Princeton and Oxford: Princeton University Press, 2005. Print.

[10] *ISAF Statistics on Attacking Species of Shark*. International Shark Attack File. Florida Museum of Natural History. University of Florida. 2014-03-19. Web. 2014-12-17.

[11] Allen, G.; Steene, R.; Humann, P.; Deloach, N.. *Reef Fish Identification: Tropical Pacific*. Jacksonville: New World Publications, 2012. Print.

[12] Lieske, E.; Myers, R. *Coral Reef Fishes: Indo-Pacific and Caribbean*. Princeton, New Jersey: Princeton University Press, 2002. Print.

[13] Folkens, P.; Reeves, R. R.; et al. *National Audubon Society: Guide to Marine Mammals of the World*. Alfred A. Knopf, 2002. Print.

[14] Haywood, M.; Wells, S. *The Interpret Manual of Marine Invertebrates*. London, New York: Salamander Books Limited: 1989. Print.

[15] Cunningham, P.; Goetz, P. *Venomous and Toxic Marine Life of the World*. Houston, Texas: Pisces Books, 1996. Print.

[16] Gershwin, L.-A. *Stung! On Jellyfish Blooms and the Future of the Ocean*. Chicago: The University of Chicago Press, 2013. Print.

[17] Iversen, E.; Skinner, R. *Dangerous Sea Life of the West Atlantic, Caribbean, and Gulf of Mexico: A Guide for Accident Prevention and First Aid*. Sarasota: Pineapple Press, 2006. Print.

[18] *Common Hand Signals for Recreational Scuba Diving*. Recreational Scuba Training Council, Inc. (RSTC), 2005. PDF file.

[19] Thomas, D. *Seaweeds*. London: The Natural History Museum, 2002. Print.

[20] Russell, B. (Grouper and Wrasse Specialist Group). *Cheilinus Undulatus*. The IUCN Red List of Threatened Species. 2014-03. Web. 2015-01-03.

[21] Collette, B.; Amorim, A. F., et al. *Thunnus Thynnus*. The IUCN Red List of Threatened Species. 2014-03. Web. 2015-01-03.

[22] Ruppert, E.; Fox, R.; Barnes, R. *Invertebrate Zoology (7th edition)*. Pacific Grove: Brooks Cole Publishing, 2004. Print.

[23] Spalding, M.; Ravilious, C.; Green, E. *World Atlas of Coral Reefs*. Berkeley: University of California Press, 2001. Print.

[24] Achituv, Y.; Dubinsky, Z. *Evolution and Zoogeography of Coral Reefs: Ecosystems of the World*. Amsterdam: Elsevier, 1990. Print.

[25] *Giant Clam: Tridacna Gigas*. Animals Database. National Geographic Society. Web. 2014-12-21.

[26] Bergbauer, M.; Myers, R.; Kirschner, M. *Das Kosmos Handbuch: Gefährliche Meerestiere*. Stuttgart: Kosmos Verlag, 2008. Print.

[27] Write, B. *Alaska's Great White Sharks*. Top Predator Publishing Company, 2007. Print.

[28] Bass, A. J.; D'Aubrey, J. D.; Kistnasamy, N. "Sharks of the East Coast of Southern Africa." *Invest. Rep. Oceanogr. Res. Inst.*, Durban, 33 (1973). Print.

[29] Froese, R.; Pauly, D. (eds.) *Anarchias Leucurus*. FishBase. January 2010. Web. 2014-12-23.

[30] Froese, R.; Pauly, D. (eds.) *Strophidon Sathete*. FishBase. January 2010. Web. 2014-12-23.

[31] Campbell, E. *Large Grouper*. Scubadoc's Diving Medicine Online. 2010-07-10. Web. 2014-12-23.

[32] *Angelfish*. Wikipedia, The Free Encyclopedia. Wikimedia Foundation, Inc. 2014-12-10 . Web. 2014-12-25.

[33] *Drum*. Encyclopaedia Britannica Online. 2013-09-07 . Web. 2015-02-22.

[34] *Stromateidae*. Wikipedia, The Free Encyclopedia. Wikimedia Foundation, Inc. 2014-05-25. Web. 2014-12-25.

[35] Robins, C. R.; Ray, G. C. *A Field Guide to Atlantic Coast Fishes of North America*. Boston: Houghton Mifflin Company, 1986. Print.

[36] Videlier, H.; Geertjes, G. J. and Videlier, J. J. "Biochemical Characteristics and Antibiotic Properties of the Mucous Envelope of the Queen Parrotfish." *Journal of Fish Biology*, 54 (1999): 1124—1127. Print.

[37] Glenday, C. (ed). *Guinness World Records 2009*. New York: Bantam Books, 2009. Print.

[38] Burton, M.; Burton, R.. *International Wildlife Encyclopedia: Tree Squirrel–Water Spider*. Singapore: Marshall Cavendish, 2002. Print.

[39] Block, B. A.; Booth, D.; Carey, F. "Direct Measurement of Swimming Speeds and Depth of Blue Marlin." *Journal of Experimental Biology*, 166 (1992): 267–284. Print.

[40] *Sea Turtle*. Wikipedia, The Free Encyclopedia. Wikimedia Foundation, Inc. 2014-12-18. Web. 2014-12-29.

[41] *Sea Snake*. Wikipedia, The Free Encyclopedia. Wikimedia Foundation, Inc. 2014-12-27. Web. 2014-12-29.

Index

Abort action, 29
Above, 11
Again, 30
Aggressive, 81
Air
    give, 19
    low on…, 18
    out of…, 18
Air pressure, 32
    in bars, 32
    in PSI, 35
    technical diving, 35
Anemone, 38
Anemonefish, 59
Angelfish, 55
Anglerfish, 70
Arc, 79
Ascend, 8
    a little, 31
    to level, 8
Ascend, exit this way, 15
Attention, 29

Bannerfish, 64
    masked, 64
Barracuda, 53
Batfish, 63
Battery
    full, 91
    full?, 91
    half-full, 91
    low, 92
Below, 11
Big, 84
Bind, 89
Bitten, 21
Blacktip reef shark, 48

Bleeding, 22
Bluespotted Ribbontail Ray, 45
Bluespotted Stingray, 45
Boat, 14
Boring, 83
Boxfish, 56
Breathe, 28
Bridge, 79
Broken, 92
Bubbles
    big, 25
    tiny, 26
Buddy, 30
Bull shark, 49
Butterfish, 57
Butterflyfish, 63

Calm down, 12
Cardinalfish, 58
Cave, 79
Ceiling, 16
Christmas tree worm, 42
Clam, 39
Cleaner shrimp, 43
Cleaning station, 80
Clownfish, 59
Cofferfish, 56
Cold, 21
Come here, 9
Cool, 82
Coral, 38
Coral reef, 80
Cornetfish, 61
Cowfish, 57
Cowry, 41

Crab, 44
Cramp, 27
Crocodile flathead, 60
Current, 77
Cut, 88

Danger
    general, 19
    over, 20
    visible, 19
Dead, 86
Decompression stop, 23
Deep, 78
Descend, 7
    to level, 8
Direction, 10
    CMAS, 11
Dizziness, 25
Dolphin, 74
Don't, 7
    touch, 90
Down, 7
Drop-off, 79
Drumfish, 58

Eagle ray, 46
Ear(s) not clearing, 20
    CMAS, 20
Eight, 36
Electric ray, 46
Emergency
    Help, 17
    Light Signal, 17
Entanglement, 24
Exercise
    begins, 29
    ends, 29
Exhaustion, 24

Exit, 15
Eyes, 9

False moorish idol, 64
Faster, 13
Fear, 23
Female, 85
Fish, 84
Five, 36
Fix, 89
Flatfish, 60
Flathead, 60
Flounder, 60
Flutemouth, 61
Follow, 13
Four, 36
Frogfish, 70

Garden eel, 54
Gather, 28
Get with your buddy, 30
Giant clam, 39
Give me air, 19
Gloves, 4
Goatfish, 59
Goosefish, 71
Grey Nurse Shark, 52
Grey reef shark, 48
Grouper, 55
Grunt, 66

Halibut, 60
Hammerhead shark, 48
Hang on, 89
Happy, 82
Hawkfish, 61
Help, 17
Hermit Crab, 44
Hold, 89
Hold hands, 12
Hover, 31

How Much air?, 32
Humphead wrasse, 73
Hurry up, 13

I, 9
I don't care, 83
I don't know, 7
In charge, 87

Jawfish, 62
Jellyfish, 38
Jetty, 79

Kelp, 37
Kneel, 28
Knife, 89

Large, 84
Lay down, 31
Lead, 13
Leak
 big, 25
 tiny, 26
Leopard shark, 49
Level off, 10
Light (Lamp), 92
Light Signal
 Emergency, 17
 Problem, 17
Line, 88
Lionfish, 67
Lobster, 43
LOL (Laugh Out Loud), 81
Longhorn Cowfish, 57
Look, 9
Lost, 27
Lost my buddy, 18
Love, 81
Low on Air, 18

Mackerel, 73
Male, 85

Manta ray, 47
Mask
 flooded, 26
 foggy, 26
Masked Bannerfish, 64
Mating, 85
Me, 9
Monkfish, 71
Moorish idol, 65
Moray eel, 54
Move apart, 31

Napoleonfish, 73
Navigate, 14
Nine, 36
Nitrogen Narcosis, 25
No, 6
No Air, 18
Numbers, 36
Nurse shark, 51

Oceanic whitetip shark, 50
Octopus, 41
OK, 4
 light signal, 5
 with gloves, 4
 with one arm, 5
 with two arms, 4
On your knees, 28
One, 36
Out of Air, 18
Over, 11

Parrotfish, 65
Photo, 90
Pick me up, 16
Pipefish, 66
Point, 15
Poisonous, 22
Poor visibility, 27
Prawn, 43

Pressure, 32
Problem, 17
    Light Signal, 17
Pufferfish, 56

Question, 6

Rabbitfish, 62
Ragged Tooth Shark, 52
Reef shark, 48
Relax, 12
Remember, 13
Repeat, 30
Rescue, 23
Rock, 78

Sad, 82
Safe, 20
Safety stop, 15
Sand, 78
Sandtiger shark, 52
Scorpionfish, 68
Sea slug, 40
Sea snail, 40
Sea snake, 75
Sea turtle, 75
Seahorse, 67
Search for, 86
Seaweed, 37
Sediment, 78
Sergeant major, 72
Seven, 36
Shallow, 77
Shark, 47
Shrimp, 43
Sick, 21
Silt out, 27
Six, 36
Sleeping, 86

Slow down, 12
Small, 84
Smile, 82
Soldierfish, 72
Sole, 60
Something is wrong, 17
Spadefish, 63
Spiny flathead, 60
Spiny lobster, 43
Sponge, 37
Squid, 42
Stay together, 30
Stingray, 45
Stone, 78
Stonefish, 68
Stop, 5
Stuck, 24
Stung, 22
Surface signal
    Help, 17
    Lost my buddy, 18
    OK (one arm), 5
    OK (two arms), 4
    Pick me up, 16
Surgeonfish, 69
Sweetlip, 66
Swim, 87
    through, 88

Take Photo, 90
Temperature, 76
    falling, 76
    rising, 76
There, 15
Thermocline, 77
Think, 13
This, 15

This way, 10
    CMAS, 11
Three, 36
Thresher shark, 51
Tiger shark, 52
Tired, 24
Touch, 90
Triggerfish, 69
Trumpetfish, 71
Tuna, 73
Turbot, 60
Turn around, 12
Turn around and swim back, 87
Two, 36

Under, 11
Unicornfish, 70
Up, 8

Venomous, 22
Vertigo, 25

Wait, 5
Watch, 9
Whale, 74
Whale shark, 53
Whatever, 83
Which way?, 10
White shark, 50
Whitetip reef shark, 48
Wreck, 14
Write it down, 16

Yes, 6

Zero, 36

SCUBA Diving Signals
The App.

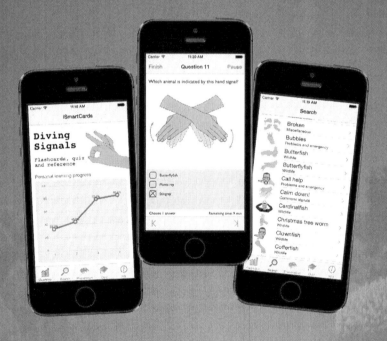

Available for iPhone and iPad

Made in the USA
Middletown, DE
31 March 2016